ALONG THE ROAD TO
SOWETO

Books by K. C. Tessendorf

LOOK OUT! HERE COMES THE STANLEY STEAMER
KILL THE TSAR!
UNCLE SAM IN NICARAGUA
BARNSTORMERS AND DAREDEVILS
ALONG THE ROAD TO SOWETO

ALONG THE ROAD TO

SOWETO

A RACIAL HISTORY OF SOUTH AFRICA

ILLUSTRATED WITH MAPS, PRINTS, AND PHOTOGRAPHS

by K. C. Tessendorf

ATHENEUM   1989   NEW YORK

Atheneum
Macmillan Publishing Company
866 Third Avenue, New York, NY 10022
Collier Macmillan Canada, Inc.
First Edition
Printed in the United States of America
10 9 8 7 6 5 4 3 2 1
Designed by Barbara A. Fitzsimmons

Library of Congress Cataloging-in-Publication Data
Tessendorf, K. C.
Along the road to Soweto: a racial history of South Africa/
by K. C. Tessendorf.—1st ed. p.   cm.   Bibliography: p.
Summary: Traces the history of South Africa from the arrival of
the Bantus 2000 years ago to the 1976 Soweto riots to the present
day. Examines race relations, the origins of apartheid, and the
different peoples who settled in South Africa.
ISBN 0-689-31401-9
1. South Africa—Race relations—Juvenile literature. 2. South
Africa—History—Juvenile literature. [1. South Africa—Race
relations. 2. South Africa—History. 3. Apartheid—South Africa.]
I. Title.
DT763.T47 1989 968—dc19
88-30535 CIP AC

To Marcia Marshall

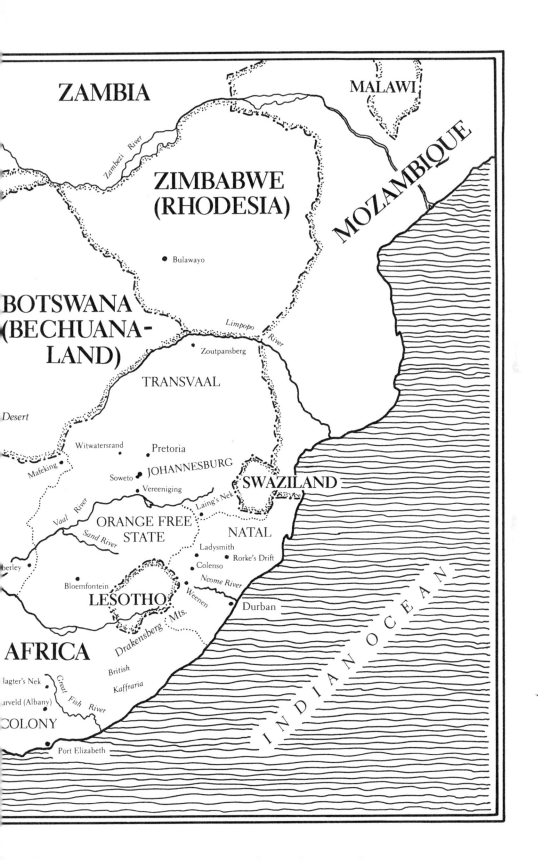

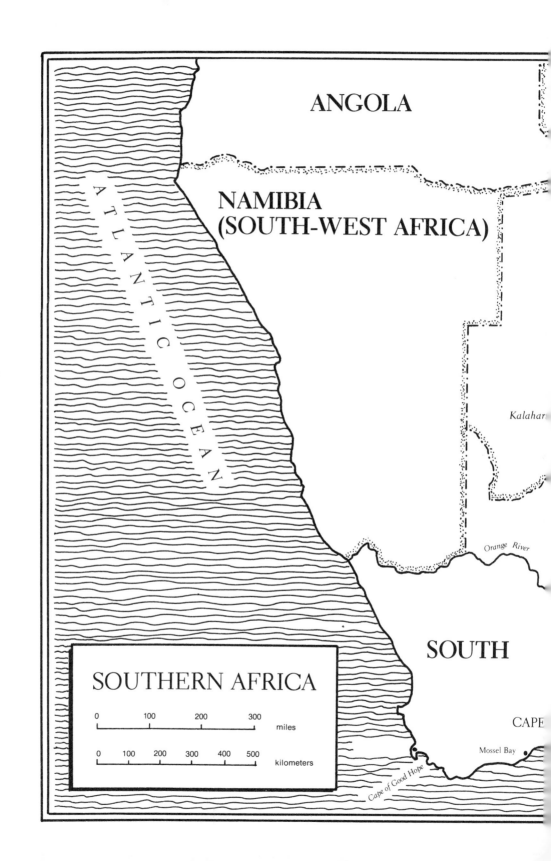

ANGOLA

NAMIBIA
(SOUTH-WEST AFRICA)

ATLANTIC OCEAN

Kalahar

Orange River

SOUTH

SOUTHERN AFRICA

0   100   200   300
miles

0   100   200   300   400   500
kilometers

CAPE

Mossel Bay

Cape of Good Hope

Contents

What is it about South Africa
that always seems to stifle reason?

J. L. DRACAPOLI

ALONG THE ROAD TO
SOWETO

INTRODUCTION

Looking into
an Unmelting Pot

Soweto, a place name that exploded into the world's moral consciousness in 1976, remains a vast, dreary, segregated black township near the city of Johannesburg, South Africa's industrial and commercial center. Enforced racial concentrations, of which Soweto is a major example, show how the country has failed to provide its multiracial peoples equal rights and opportunities.

The Republic of South Africa may be likened to a national melting pot that does not melt. Inside the pot, the varied racial ingredients have been separated and layered by events occurring over the past three hundred years. The bottom layer in the pot is black and by far the thickest. Above it are multicolored layers in hues of brown and yellow. On top is a thin layer of purest white. Though thin, it is not froth; to the contrary, it is the sealing cap over the lower layers.

It is through the labor and cooperation of the black and colored majority that the nation's daily work is done and the high standard of living continued. But these workers have been traditionally excluded from the governing process. The ruling white minority has insisted, ever more stridently after 1948, when the white Afrikaner nationality achieved political dominance, that the racial layers maintain their separations, especially socially; but on the job, too, where the whites oversee and the other races labor cheaply.

1

This strict white economic, social, and civic policy is called *apartheid* in the Afrikaans language, which is spoken by the Afrikaner whites. To accommodate apartheid, black townships like Soweto were established within commuting distance of major work sites, quarters that the inhabitants could not leave except by a pass system regulated by white magistrates.

Afrikaner apartheid advocates look back three hundred years to their justification of racial dominance and apartness, claiming that it arose from a respect for the biblically ordained order of mankind. The isolated and self-reliant Afrikaner (Boer) frontiersman of old, who faced Hottentot, Bushman, and Bantu (Zulu) tribes, found comfort and convenience in Old Testament readings about superior and inferior races. He understood it was his moral duty as a member of a superior race, living among inferior breeds, to dominate them for the welfare of all.

Twentieth-century apartheid supporters continued to claim that the "lesser breeds" under the white law were relatively happy in their places, excepting for the very few malcontents, who were likely provoked by evil outsiders.

This belief in the acceptance of apartheid by the nonwhite majority was canceled for all time by the riots that arose in Soweto in 1976. A minor issue began the confrontation. Soweto young people learned a tribal language at home, and they were taught in English in the white-run schools. But the Afrikaner element dominant in the white government then proposed to enforce a requirement that half of the studies be taught in Afrikaans, a Dutch dialect that is the language of the original white settlers. Class boycotts against this language requirement climaxed in a student demonstration where stones were thrown, and the police reacted with gunfire.

The major riot at Soweto that followed spread to similar black and colored urban concentrations across South Africa and resulted in a two-day general strike. By the time the disturbances ceased, 575 persons had been killed, nearly four thousand were injured, and thousands were arrested. National political stability was not in danger. The police response was harshly effective. Most of the casualties and all of the property damage occurred in the black and colored townships.

"Soweto," however, entered South Africa's history as a symbolic turning point. Like the Parisians' attack on the Bastille prison; like the Boston Massacre as the British troops fired into the patriot mob; or like the seemingly commonplace gesture of Mrs. Rosa Parks, the tired black lady who sat down in the whites-only section of a bus in Birmingham, Alabama, in 1955; Soweto presented notice to the world that the old order of authority and practice in South Africa was going to be changed, that the black and colored masses below the white layer in the unmelting pot were not inert and unaspiring. A process began, by civil or violent means, to melt or at least rearrange the varied racial strata. This process continues today, as frequent newspaper headlines and TV film clips affirm.

How did the government and citizens of South Africa get into this terrible, unending racial struggle? A short answer: By marching in place while the rest of the world marched onward. Indeed, after 1948, South Africa about-faced and strode in the opposite direction.

Why? There is no short answer—nor is a book-length one promised. But to know about this society's roots is to understand this tortured nation to the extent that an outsider may do so. This book considers the peoples in the unmelting pot: Who are they? What causes their distinctiveness? How did they arrive at their present condition?

1

The Road Begins

About two thousand years ago the first significant movement of people started toward what is now South Africa. Tribal groups of cattle drovers and light farmers, the Bantu peoples, then living in the West African savanna (lightly forested grassland), moved south as their population expanded.

Africa, the second largest continent, straddles the equator as a union of huge east-west and north-south land masses. It is popularly considered to be a dark and jungly place, but its rain forest is limited to the Congo River basin at Africa's equator and adjacent coastline. There is far more jungle in South America. Most of Africa is high, dry plateau with areas of mountains. The giant Sahara desert nearly fills the center of the north half, and a sizable desert, the Kalahari, lies at the northwest edge of South Africa. A major geologic trench holding a chain of large lakes reaches for thousands of miles from northeast Africa (Ethiopia) down nearly to the fringes of South Africa, forming a natural corridor for the movement of people.

Early Mediterranean civilizations settled colonies of Phoenicians, Greeks, and Romans along the North African coast, but they were shut off from the rest of Africa by the rapid expansion of the Sahara desert in those times, which also forced the Egyptians to remain close to the unfailing Nile River. The only contact between the

5

Mediterranean civilizations and black Africa south of the great desert was by way of merchant caravans.

Superior tools crafted from iron, a wonder metal to the blacks, were among the Mediterranean goods traded for slaves, gold, and ivory. A modern view is that when the Bantu learned in prehistory to forge their own iron, this new technology aided in a population explosion. With iron tools, agriculture became easier, forest clearing was quicker, and iron weapons gave superiority on the battlefield. So, expanded in population and pressed by the Sahara desert creeping down from the north, the Bantu peoples pushed through Stone Age tribes in a slow migration south through the rain forest and east to the head of the lakes below the Ethiopian mountains, and pressed south via the long lakes corridor.

The migrants, their population steadily increasing, probably crossed the Zambesi River, the major stream on Africa's east slope, before A.D. 1000. South Africa's southeast coast was reached during the next five hundred years.

The Bantu who arrived in South Africa were tall and strongly built, with a well-developed tribal organization and skill at cattle droving and crop cultivation. For centuries they had been pushing into territory inhabited by another culture, the San people (Bushmen). The San were primitive hunters without an oral history or tribal development who lived in nomadic family groups. Of yellowish color, the diminutive San grew to about four feet in height, with prominent stomach and buttocks. Their technical achievement was the poisoned arrow.

The Bushmen held no concept of private property. To them a cow was as good a target as a zebra and more easily taken, so the San hunting clans persistently raided any available cattle herd. For this the Bushmen were universally hated and hunted to the edge of extinction, by cattle-herding blacks—and whites. A few hundred presently survive on a reservation in the Kalahari desert.

In the west and southwest of South Africa lived the Khoi-khoi (Hottentot) people. Also yellow-brown and somewhat Asian in fea-

A group of Bushmen in an early print.

tures, they were cattle herders associated in tribes, but they had not acquired the skills of working iron, nor did they farm. Their origin is guessed to be a mixture of Bantu and San. The Khoi-khoi arrived in the south unknown centuries ahead of the Bantu, probably also displacing or exterminating the resident Bushmen. The Khoi-khoi, as a distinctive people, were absorbed by white invaders, debased, enslaved, and killed off by foreign disease. Few if any pure-blood Hottentots remain today.

How about the other major people of the future South Africa? When the Bantu began their migration, their future antagonists, the Dutch and the English, were barbarian tribes benefiting from their conquest by Rome.

The far tip of Africa lies about seven thousand miles (twice the distance to North America) south of London and about a third farther by ship route. Vessels were small and the southern seas unknown. Not until after A.D. 1400 did Europeans venture on sea voyages south of Gibraltar.

For a thousand years, the slow evolution of European nations from feudal fiefdoms was disturbed by migrations, raids, and attacks by outsiders: Angles, Saxons, Vikings, Mongols, and Muslims. Africa, to the medieval European, surely appeared to be a dark continent, the lair of the fierce Islamic Moors.

In these times a studious brother of the Portuguese king Prince Henry the Navigator looked toward Africa as the key to global navigation. There were fabled riches in the black nations south of the great desert; and where might the venturesome sailor sail in the unknown seas below? Prince Henry knew of the tradition that claimed Phoenicians had sailed east to west *around* Africa two thousand years ago. If that were true, Portugal, by sailing south and east, could reach and secure the wealth of the Indies.

Few believed in Prince Henry's vision, but he benefited from his royal connection. So, beginning about 1418, successive seafaring expeditions probed farther down Africa's barren west coast. They turned Africa's westward bulge at Cape Verde in 1444; and Portuguese hopes were high as they advanced eastward and began carrying back cargos of slaves, ivory, and gold from the populous coastal native kingdoms. But after the mouth of the Congo River near the equator was passed, the African continent again stretched on south and became uninteresting, vacant desert coastline again.

Prince Henry died, but the expeditions stubbornly continued southward against contrary winds and currents. João II was on the Portuguese throne, and this king also held to an Indies vision. Like many other wishful Europeans, he believed in the all-powerful eastern Christian monarch, "Prester John," and planned to send Portugal's ships to link with this mighty king. Together they might defeat Islam, and, meanwhile, the Portuguese would reward themselves

Portuguese sea explorers seeking the kingdom of the legendary Prester John were drawn southward toward "Etiopia" by old African maps like this Venetian specimen.

with the wealth of the Indies, too. Little Portugal wanted to have it all!

But Prester John was a myth, a three-hundred-year-old fraud. In 1177, the pope in Rome received a faked letter from a nonexistent Christian monarch of the Indies, announcing grandly that "As Prester John, I am lord of lords. Under heaven, I surpass in riches and virtue and power all other kings upon the whole earth." Over the following centuries, papal envoys and European commercial travelers, including Marco Polo, scouted among the declining Christian colonies in Persia, India, even Mongolia, but didn't find Prester John. They decided he had never been.

But Christian Europe, wishfully preferring to believe in this exotic champion of Christianity in the East, preserved the dream by transferring the legend to Africa. Prester John became in Western lore the all-powerful black Christian king of inaccessible Ethiopia. If only he could be reached and his aid enlisted, all would go well. And it was upon this hope that the Portuguese João II acted.

The king invoked a dual strategy. His sea adventurers were to keep pushing their vessels southward until they passed around Africa or found an overland shortcut. When the Congo River was discovered, eager Portuguese sailed up the mighty stream, hoping it led to his kingdom. Meanwhile, João II commissioned a two-man spy mission to secretly cross Islam, visit Prester John, and explore the Indies.

At this time, far south of the equator, the king's seafaring explorer, Bartolemeu Dias, was pressing south into the unknown along Africa's monotonous desert coast when a series of storms blew the Portuguese in their small ship west and south for thirteen days. The mariners then found themselves in a fearful sea environment. The temperature had turned markedly cold, and wind howled across gray and heaving seas. They had entered the latitudes that future sailors would respectfully call "the roaring forties."

Dias steered east for the haven of the desert continent and sailed and sailed without seeing Africa on the wave-tossed horizon. Desperately, he turned due north and gratefully came in sight of a land mass lying east-west. The rejoicing Portuguese came to this green coast at a river's mouth and saw a large herd of cattle tended by natives. At sight of the seaborne apparition, the cattle stampeded into the hills, herded by the frightened Khoi-khoi. Cape Vacca (cows), South Africa, was the point of this 1488 Portuguese discovery of the continent's end, with its promise of a passage to the Indies.

Dias turned east along this windy coast and at Mossel Bay landed and met the Khoi-khoi, trading metal trinkets for fresh meat. Dias noted these natives were chestnut-brown, not tall, clothed in sheepskins, and wore bracelets of ivory and elephant's hair. Soon something disturbed the Khoi-khoi that sign language could not rectify. The natives withdrew a short distance and then showered the Portuguese with stones. In anger, Dias took up a crossbow and impulsively killed a native, after which both parties withdrew in a hurry.

A few days later on the eastward course, the captain faced the threat of crew mutiny. So Dias regretfully turned back for Portugal, knowing he had discovered the Indies passage. Rounding the headland at Africa's southwest corner, he named the cape Bon Esperance, Good Hope for Portugal's rich future in the Indies. But it was nine years before the follow-up expedition of Vasco da Gama passed the cape during its historic round-trip to India. Why the delay?

The king was waiting for word from Prester John! João II's spies passed through Egypt, down the Red Sea to Aden, and separated. Afonso de Paiva's mission was to contact Prester John, but Paiva died en route to Ethiopia. Meanwhile, his companion explored the rim of the Indian Ocean with success. Pero da Covilha was among the most remarkable incognito travelers of history.

Still a young man, he had already shown his talent for deception in three secret missions for his king into Spain and Moorish North Africa. An observant and highly adaptable traveler, Covilha's knowledge of Muslim language and custom was exact. He never blew his cover. In the pose of a well-traveled Arab merchant, the Portuguese spy crossed the Arabian sea in a dhow, an Arabic boat, landing upon India's spice coast. Having acquainted himself to the trade there, Covilha passed over to the Persian port of Hormuz, where the westbound caravans assembled. Then, hearing of a great gold source three thousand miles away in southeast Bantu Africa (King Solomon's Mines), the intrepid observer managed to cross the Indian Ocean to visit in turn each of the Arab slave-trading stations along the East African coast down to Mozambique and the great island of Madagascar. At the farthest south mainland station of Sofala, he was assured that a sea passage around Africa was certainly there.

Filled with exotic intelligence after three years of purposeful travel, Covilha was in Egypt again en route to Portugal when he was contacted by Portuguese emissaries with instructions for him from João II: Don't return without contacting Prester John. So the faithful spy wrote out a valuable, detailed intelligence report about his travels, which one of the emissaries carried back to the king. Covilha then escorted the other newcomer on a tour to India and Persia. Afterward crossing Saudi Arabia alone en route to Ethiopia, Covilha paused as perhaps the first European to visit Islam's holy shrine of Mecca.

Covilha traveled on and successfully entered the mountain citadel of Ethiopia's Coptic Christian kingdom, where he revealed himself as Portugal's Christian ambassador. He found a pleasant land of culture, but no rich all-powerful ally against Islam. While Covilha lingered there, his expertise as a man of the world solved a royal Ethiopian dynastic crisis. His hosts then gave him a fine estate and awarded him a lovely princess, but told him that he could never leave their kingdom! And so it was that thirty years later, Portuguese missionaries penetrated Ethiopia and found Pero da Covilha still living a pampered life of enforced exile.

Back in Portugal, the waiting for further intelligence from Pero da Covilha stretched into years. João II died, and his successor, Manuel I, also waited for word on Prester John. Finally, in 1497, Vasco da Gama was sent out on the historic voyage round-trip to India by way of the Portuguese colony of Brazil and South and East Africa. Passing the Bantu-populated east coast of South Africa at Christmas, da Gama named it Natal, or birth. Likely using the ten-year-old report of Covilha, the royal captain called at Arab ports along East Africa, always asking for knowledge of Prester John, and receiving "farther on" replies of no substance. Finally crossing to India, de Gama loaded on a fortune in silks and spices. After that, Portuguese power and wealth controlled the South African route.

Having established refreshment stations, which provided fresh food to prevent scurvy, on the south Atlantic island of St. Helena and at Mozambique in southeast Africa, the Portuguese mainly bypassed South Africa. The coast was stormy, and there was no evidence that the land held treasure. Even occasional calls there for fresh beef halted after 1510. In that year the Portuguese governor in the East Indies, Francisco de Almeida, was returning to Portugal

The Portuguese explorer Vasco da Gama passed the Cape of Good Hope and named the land Natal, as he captained the first European ship to visit the Indies and return home safely (1497–99).

in triumph, following great military and trade victories. His fleet paused at Table Bay, Cape of Good Hope, for fresh water and meat.

The local Khoi-khoi seemed unusually friendly, and the small landing party of sailors felt encouraged to visit their village a mile or two inland. After arriving, though, the visitors were stripped of knives, buckles, and buttons by the acquisitive natives, who afterward went with the Portuguese to their ships. Near the beach a fight broke out in which one of the sailors was bloodily beaten.

The next day the vengeful Portuguese landed a military expedition of 150 men, including de Almeida and most of his captains, who marched to the Khoi-khoi village. Most of the natives fled ahead, but the invaders found some children in the huts and planned to abduct them. Then:

> *About eighty of the negroes came down from the place they had taken refuge in the first moment of terror, as men ready to face death to save their children. . . .*

> *Having called their cattle, which are accustomed to this kind of warfare, they began to whistle to them, and make signs by which they guide them, so that forming into a squadron, and sheltered by the cattle, they attacked our men with darts hardened by fire. Some fell wounded and were trodden down by the cattle, and as most of them were without shields, their only weapons being lances and swords, in this kind of warfare they could not do much damage to the negroes.*

The retreat became a rout, a run for the beach. But the Portuguese ships had moved offshore due to a heavy ground swell.

> *They sank in the sand of the shore, and were entirely powerless and unable to move, and the negroes came down upon them so light-footed and nimble that they appeared to be birds, or rather the devil's executioners.*

Sixty-five Portuguese, including Governor de Almeida and most of his proud captains, were slaughtered. Thereafter the Portuguese steered clear of the South African coasts, and the Khoi-khoi gained a final one hundred years of peace.

2

The Dutch
"Tavern of the Seas"

Throughout the sixteenth century, the Portuguese profited immensely from their Indies trade. The rich, exotic cargos were resold on the docks of Lisbon to European distributors, principally the Dutch. But when the Protestant Reformation divided Christian Europe after 1525, the Dutch people, strongly Protestant, fought to free themselves from their Catholic overlords in Spain. The coastal provinces of Holland became independent by 1581.

At the same time, Portugal received a new king from Spain, Philip II, who shortsightedly closed the port of Lisbon to Dutch shipping. The Dutch then went out and traded directly in the Indies, followed by the English and French, as the Portuguese market faded. Ships from each of these countries now occasionally stopped along the South African coasts.

The Khoi-khoi considered themselves rather agreeably well set up in South Africa. They were self-sufficient in an economy based upon the products of their cattle and sheep, animals they did not customarily slaughter for meat. They lived a good life by their standards and were unafflicted by other's ambitions.

To these people, the periodic appearance of the strangers from the sea was a circus spectacle and a beach bazaar. The Khoi-khoi were attracted to the metal curios, strips, and pieces, especially brass, that the visitors proposed to barter for cattle. And they received a rare and bountiful feast when the strangers slaughtered livestock on the beach and gave back these "best parts" savored by the Khoi-khoi, who, like the majestic Cape lions, preferred the abdominal organs above all steaks.

Had they understood the purpose of the foreigners' voyaging past their shores to the ends of the earth—that it was merely to obtain

A Khoi-khoi couple, from a seventeenth-century English engraving, which shows a child nursing over the shoulder, as the mother exhibits an intestine delicacy.

spices so that the Europeans could look and smell good—these natives would have been even more derisive of crazy alien customs. Khoi-khoi grooming involved smearing one's body with cow dung, drying it in the sun, then peeling—the Hottentot bath. Next they rubbed rancid animal fat spiced with herbal flavors over all parts and, lastly, sprinkled the whole with powder ground from the local heather bloom.

Khoi-khoi religious and social mores were easygoing, their philosophy one of getting by. Actually, in the time of settlement, it took some effort by the Europeans to corrupt and thereby control the happy, self-sufficient Hottentots.

Sir Thomas Smythe was an English merchant-adventurer seeking profits in the age of exploration. Smythe began with the Virginia Company in North America, a land without the fabulous wealth of the Indies, and was able to make a profit from tobacco plantations. Sir Thomas wondered if he could make money trading on the Saldanian coasts, as the southwest Cape of Good Hope area was then called.

He sent down a ship in 1613. Captain Gabriel Towerson established contact with the local Khoi-khoi tribe, but was frustrated in gaining any information because of the very difficult "clicky" language. A man of action, Towerson lured the local chief and an associate aboard his ship, kidnapped them, and sailed for England!

Though well treated, the Khoi-khoi were distressed enough to undertake a hunger strike from which the associate died. But Xhore, the chief, decided to live and cooperate, even to accepting English baths and clothing. Whatever his thoughts were when he stood on the deck as the vessel moved up the Thames River to medieval London, or later as the socially proper guest and student in the fine town house of Sir Thomas Smythe, he did not reveal them to his hosts. The great merchant made much of his intelligent, exotic captive and perhaps presented him to James I and his court. Sir Thomas, told of the Khoi-khoi weakness for brass, had a shining suit of that metal tailored for Xhore (called Coree because the English

The following text appears within the engraving:

VERA EFFIGIES PRÆCLARISS.MI VIRI DOM.INI THOMÆ SMITH EQVITIS AVRATI ETC.

Simon Paſſeus ſculp: Lond: A°.1617. Compt: Holland excud

The honourable S.r Thomas Smith Knight, late Embaſ-
ador from his Ma.tie to y.e great Emperour
of Ruſſie, Gouernour of y.e Hon.ble and famous
Societyes of Marcha.nts tradinge to y.e Eaſt-
Indies, Muſcovy, the French and Somer-
Ilands Company: Treſurer for Virginia.etc.

The English merchant-adventurer Sir Thomas Smythe, who settled convicts
at the Cape and hosted the Khoi-khoi chieftain Xhore.

could not manage the click X), who was very pleased.

The native chief, about thirty years old, learned broken English, but he didn't satisfy his hosts with what they sought—commercial information about his homeland. Instead, the grieving exile repeatedly prostrated himself before Sir Thomas, kissing his boots, all the while crying out, "Xhore, go home—Saldania, go!"

So Xhore, with his splendid brass outfit, returned to Saldanian shores. The English hoped that he would at least become their contact and ally in the strange southern land. But, instead, he walked with his people into the interior and was not seen again by his patrons, though he did send back cattle to be traded to them.

Future voyagers to those parts described him as completely reverted to Khoi-khoi culture. With his English and knowledge of the true value of European products, though, he became a disagreeably hard bargainer.

But Sir Thomas persisted in his venture, and now he readied his prisoner plan: Hanging was the appropriate penalty, in medieval England, for even the commonest felonies, like purse snatching. There was, however, an off-and-on practice of pardoning the condemned if they agreed to do a job overseas that no free citizen would consider.

That is how Sir Thomas Smythe found ten men to be put ashore in Saldania and left there on their own as observers for a season or more. The selected ones, who had opted for any life rather than death, sailed for South Africa in 1615 with an English East Indies merchant fleet, a voyage that consumed much time and allowed two of the more personable convicts to persuade high officials aboard to take them on to the Indies as personal servants.

The remaining eight were put ashore at the Cape of Good Hope under the command of Captain John Crosse, a man of wild temperament who had provoked too many duels, resulting in his discharge as a king's guard officer. He earned his date with the hangman by becoming a highwayman afterward. But Crosse ashore also failed to control his temper and soon was murdered by natives, probably of

Xhore's tribe. It is recorded that he was stuck like a pincushion.

The group had been left a rowboat, and in it the remaining seven fled to an offshore island, called in Welsh *pen-guin* (white heads) and occupied by these flightless birds, but by little else. The refugees wrecked their boat in landing and so were marooned. For months they suffered near starvation until a ship appeared in the bay.

Four of the castaways couldn't wait and built a raft from their boat wreckage to go to the vessel. But they miscalculated the tide and were turned about in midpassage to drift helplessly out to sea. The three more prudent survivors were picked up and carried back to England. They spent much time en route in stocks because they had reverted to criminal behavior. When the ship arrived in an English harbor, the three dived overboard and swam ashore. Cold, wet, and hungry, they soon committed robberies, were afterward captured, and were speedily hanged!

Sir Thomas, meanwhile, had sent down two other separate trios of gallows birds. The first three, when they heard of Saldania in detail, approached their ship captain and passionately begged to be hanged from the yardarm rather than be put ashore. The captain relented and carried them onward to India. The other three went ashore in true-blue style, but were never heard from again. No more prisoners were sent to Saldania; instead, they were routed to Smythe interests in Virginia and the Bahamas.

It is said that Xhore, some years later, relayed to Sir Thomas a proposal offering open trade. In exchange he wanted military aid and the construction of an English-style house. But other interests then occupied the merchant's business attention. In 1625 Smythe died, and English dabbling at the Cape ended for a while.

In the seventeenth century, it was the turn of the Dutch to prosper in the Indies. Unlike the Portuguese, who based themselves on the coast of India, the Dutch founded their trading center at Batavia, Java (now Jakarta, Indonesia), a very long sea haul across the southern Indian Ocean. Then, in 1647, the *Haarlem,* a company ship bound home with a cargo of Indies wealth, wrecked near the

Cape of Good Hope. Since the riches were salvageable, about half the crew remained to oversee it for the half-year or so before another pick-up vessel could come. The stranded sailors were able to cultivate garden vegetables and also to get on well with the local Khoi-khoi.

Scurvy was, in those times, a common debilitating and fatal disease of vitamin C deficiency, certain to appear aboard vessels that were at sea for long periods. A voyage from Holland to Java consumed six or more months. A midpoint refreshment station was needed, so the Dutch East Indies Company, acting on the encouraging *Haarlem* report, decided to establish a facility at the Cape of Good Hope in the no-man's-land of South Africa.

The company had definite ideas about the mission of its future Cape station. A small, economical complement, less than one hundred employees, would be sent down to build a fort and a small surrounding town, to plant vegetables and fruit trees, and to trade with the Khoi-khoi to establish company cattle and sheep herds. Certainly friendly relations needed to be maintained with the local people, since they were the sole source of meat on the hoof. The natives were also scheduled to become cheap laborers for the company. The usual inducements of trinkets, tobacco, and arrack (rice brandy) would be used to keep the savages happy and addicted to being useful.

Though a profit could hardly be expected from the way station, it would follow good Dutch sense and thrift in servicing the Indies fleets with antiscurvy groceries of fresh greens, beef, and mutton during the vessels' ten-day stopover. Foreign ships were to be resupplied, too, paying premium rates.

Generally, it was hoped that the Cape station would function as well as the trading post called New Amsterdam, which the sister West Indies Company operated on the tip of an island called Manhattan in the wilds of North America. A lesson to be learned from that enterprise was that colonists not employed by the company soon became unruly, flouting regulations. A group of Boers (farmers) had soon gone off a few miles into the Manhattan forest and formed their own settlement, known as the *boery* (bowery). So the Dutch East Indies Company ruled out a colony at the Cape; it was to be solely a company installation.

Johan Van Riebeeck, thirty-three, was the company man selected to found and govern the Cape station. Van Riebeeck's earlier promising career in the Dutch East Indies had been blighted by his recall for using the company facility to profit personally. He had made his amends at headquarters and was eager to go out again from Holland to even a third-rate assignment like South Africa, for to be successful there might mean that he could get out to Batavia again.

On Christmas Eve 1651, he and eighty company personnel (including four wives) departed from Holland, and after a tolerable

The first Dutch colonists bargain with the Khoi-khoi.

Johan Van Riebeeck, founding governor of the Cape Colony for the Dutch East Indies Company.

voyage of three-and-a-half months, landed at the windy bay below the Cape's distinctive Table Mountain. April 6, 1652, saw the founding of Capetown, South Africa.

For quite a while nothing went according to plan. The settlement was founded amid oncoming winter gales, which blew away the Dutchmen's gardens as soon as they appeared. Baboon troops were reported as nasty neighbors, and local leopards became adept poultry thieves, along with the two-legged native variety.

The most severe and significant disappointment related to the Khoi-khoi, now called Hottentots after the Dutch word for stammerer. The local tribesmen were scroungy beachcombers without cattle or sheep. They had to be coaxed into acting as shifty middlemen in dealings with inland cattle-owning Hottentots. Four months passed before any livestock were obtained. It was also plain that the happy-go-lucky Hottentots were not about to work dependably for the strangers.

The Dutch had come to stay and would do whatever seemed necessary to bolster their presence. The Hottentot's lackadaisical attitude toward trade with the white invaders induced the disgusted, worried Governor Van Riebeeck to request, within six weeks of arrival, a change in company policy. Unless the company was willing to send down hired European laborers, an expense the governor well knew it did not want to undertake, Van Riebeeck proposed slavery—not of the Hottentots, but from abroad, in the standard seventeenth-century pattern.

Human bondage had flourished from the time men realized that it was smarter to make strangers work for them than to kill their captives. Enslavement became the norm, the result and proof of tribal or national defeat. The Old Testament patriarchs considered it a natural condition, and in New Testament Roman times, Saint Paul acknowledged the institution. Europeans, who in their feudal system exercised near-total control over their peasants' lives, turned to it easily when they settled tropical America in a plantation economy of sugar, tobacco, and cotton.

West Africa was, for Europe, the handiest source geographically, with plenty of slaves for sale, but similar markets could be found in East Africa, where Arabs had been slave brokers for at least a thousand years; the condition was common also in India and southeast Asia. To the slight extent that slave traders and buyers justified their business, they claimed purchases saved lives that would otherwise be terminated (avoiding the fact that buyer demand caused and expanded enslavement). Also, it was virtuously asserted that the slaves of Europeans would be better off in a culture of Christian enlightenment.

The Dutch East Indies Company was deep into slaveholding. Its Indies operations rested upon the labor of Malaysian and other slaves. So Van Riebeeck got permission to import slaves as a company monopoly. Hottentots were excluded, for the company still counted on their cattle and sheep resources.

It took some time for the governor to gather slaves into his out-of-the-way station. The first were "two little Arab girls" given by a passing French admiral; a few Malaysians trickled in from the Dutch Indies. Then a Portuguese slave ship was captured by a company fleet, and the Cape Colony received about 170 black children and teenagers taken from Angola. There were early good intentions to educate, Christianize, and eventually liberate individuals. But this attitude did not long survive the crass commercialism at the Cape.

Next, a shipload of 228 slaves was purchased on the "slave coast" of West Africa, but problems with runaways taught the colonists it was better to put wide water between the slave and his or her homeland, and future slaves came from Madagascar, India's Bengal coast, Malaysia, and Indo China. An attempt to purchase slaves up the nearby coast failed because the Bantu chiefs refused to sell their Bantu captives. They reasoned that these white strangers who slaughtered every cow or sheep they could get in hand should not be trusted. The Bantu suspected the Dutch were cannibals!

The efficient Dutch soon noted that it required three slaves to do the work expected by European standards from one laborer. And soon there were no European laborers and few white craftsmen remaining in the Cape work force; for they, through economics and cultural pride, had withdrawn before cheap and available slaves. Even a middle-class city family might own a dozen or more. The white's share of *doing work* was eased to near zero. There was sloth at the top, and even the slave mass didn't work all that hard. Baron Van Imhoff, a high official of the efficiency-intensive Dutch East Indies Company, noted in 1717:

> *I believe it would have been far better, had we, when this colony was founded, commenced with Europeans and brought them thither in such numbers that hunger and want would have forced them to work. But having imported slaves, every common or ordinary European becomes a gentleman and prefers to be served than to serve. . . . We have in addition . . . that the majority of farmers in this colony are not farmers in the real sense of the word, but owners of plantations, and that many of them consider it a shame to work with their own hands.*

Slavery in South Africa, ended by 1834, never exceeded a resident population of forty thousand slaves, but the habits begun through slavery in early Cape Colony endure into the present day. That is to say, generally, the whites supervise a cheap, plentiful labor force of other races.

The other modern condition created by the importation of slaves into the small, vulnerable Cape station is the mixed-race class that had its beginning in the early days of slaveholding. Members of this mixed-racial subculture became known as the Cape Coloured, and they presently form about sixteen percent of South Africa's population.

During the century and a half when the Cape area was governed by the Dutch East Indies Company, the diverse slave nationalities mixed with little discrimination, and with the white settlers as well. Nearly all of the early company employees were bachelors, and cultural bars between the races were of serious concern only when property was affected. Meanwhile, shore-leave sailors of every nationality on earth crowded into Capetown, "the tavern of the seas."

The company law followed the Roman standard: The offspring of free men and slave women took on the servitude of the mother. Half-white slaves were more valuable, both in their owner's estimation, and in bringing a higher price when sold. It is recorded that an ambitious slave entrepreneur employed "an Irishman . . . to no other purpose than to improve his stock." South African historian Victor de Kock avows that: "Any 17th century burgher could live for years with a slave girl and then, should he tire of her, he could sell the mother and also the children he had procreated by her." White parentage of slave children was high in early times at the Cape—by one claim seventy-five percent!

Capetown, the popular "tavern of the seas," was a roistering port-of-call like many others, though likely more efficiently operated since it was Dutch. The most boisterous time was when the return company fleet arrived from Batavia, inbound to Holland. "Wild and obstreperous" crewmen then terrorized Capetown. A traveler recalls their arrival in an early year when there were only about two hundred inhabitants of the place:

> They trod underfoot and crushed all the vegetables in the Garden; drove the gardeners away with knives and stones; burned the Company's boat, a sampan, as well as wheelbarrows and other such objects that came within their reach; carried off pigs, fowls, ducks, doors and window-frames; . . . persuaded more than a quarter of the full quota of residents to stow away in the ships, and merrily ended a busy and boisterous day by setting upon the settlement's one and only policeman and chasing that discomfited official from house to house.

Capetown's popularity often exceeded its resources. More vegetables, and especially more beef and mutton, could have been supplied to company ships, or could have been profitably sold to others, if they could have been provided. This annoyed the parent company, and by extension became a serious headache for the first governors. It led to the breaking of the second basic company rule: the barring of independent colonists.

The Hottentots had no interest in increasing their herds to meet Dutch demands, but a growing native thirst for Dutch brandy and a desire for tobacco influenced them to trade more of their livestock to the Dutch. Since the cattle sellers took no steps to replace their herds, they inevitably thinned out.

Governor Van Riebeeck understood that the company would have to build and maintain its own herds. But employees in the let-the-slaves-do-it atmosphere couldn't meet the need. Personal profit was a strong motivator, Van Riebeeck remembered, and he thought of the independent farmers (Boers) back in Holland, who were ambitious and would make good on a opportunity to get ahead. So the Dutch East Indies Company reluctantly agreed to recruit and send down a trial group; they also allowed the governor to release from company employment a few interested men already serving at the Cape.

The Boers arrived on company ships after a free passage from Holland; stolid, intelligent, hardworking Dutch and Germans, Calvinist by religion. The settlers had agreed to produce and sell livestock and agricultural products from their own farms exclusively to the company and to abide by its manifold rules of civil and business conduct.

The newcomers fulfilled their agreements, so others were sent down, including a batch of Huguenots. These Protestant refugees from Catholic France introduced the production of wines and brandies to the Cape economy. By the early eighteenth century, there were several hundred self-reliant and successful Boers pushing the colony's borders out into the crop and grassland, displacing Hottentots who scarcely troubled to fight about it.

But along with the producing, the Boers created new problems for the company. In Europe they had been independent farmers, who were free of a castle lord's commands. Now they were individually engaged in taming a wild new land, and were very free in interpreting the fussy rules of the company.

Most alarming, in Capetown's view, was their desire to move into the unknown hinterland. Out of sight meant out of control. The company worried that the wanderers would start a war with the natives. War would increase expenses while suspending trade and profits!

3

The English Become the Bane of the Boers

History remembers no Boer sailors or fishermen. They were land men, generations of farmers, skilled and free, who had been cooped up on small European acreages and who now looked toward a limitless and empty (natives didn't count) continental interior. Just beyond Capetown lay an agricultural plain climbing to grasslands backed by mountain ridges that were snowcapped in winter. By 1715, many would be living in contentment beyond sight of the smoke of their nearest neighbor.

The Dutch farmers, who penetrated the first mountain ridges beyond Capetown, changed their life-styles forever, for the land there could not support intensive agriculture.

It was suited, and had long been used, as pastureland by cattle- and sheepherding Hottentots and Bantus. Rainfall was uncertain, veering between just enough and not enough, better in the east than in the west. The weather and poor soil limited settled grazing, but the climate was a healthy one for Europeans, and the first individuals in the Boers' expansion easily adapted to these conditions. They became wanderers, sharing the interior velds (grasslands) with the native livestock owners, and soon dominated them.

The Dutch East Indies Company's restrictions on the travels of the "trekboers" was a failure from the start. The demands of back-

31

country living had no relevance to the rules published by the company. They were quietly ignored or abused to Boer purposes. The few officials sent into the backlands usually adjusted to the views of the local whites. While the trekboers did much as they pleased, they did deliver the expected increase in livestock to the company monopoly.

So at length the company encouraged the trekboers to expand without capital investment. "Loan farms" of their choice were made available, nearly six thousand acres for a yearly rent of the equivalent of twenty-five dollars, with an option to move out and rent another spread at any time. The variable climate and land conditions easily caused overgrazing, which meant, inevitably, expansion into fresh, new land. For a century, company policy made this easy. Out on the frontier, Boers might not bother to register their whereabouts, or remember to remit rent to the distant company. It was unlikely they'd ever meet a nosy official.

Gradually the most distant trekboers assumed a subsistence land culture not greatly different from that of surrounding native herdsmen. Once over the first ridge into a roadless countryside, they could not market field crops. Though cattle and sheep were walked to market, as the decades passed, the real frontiersmen moved out too far to trade regularly with Capetown.

By 1800, six or more generations raised in this cultural isolation produced the self-assured, self-reliant Boer. These taciturn, resilient plainsmen and women knew and cared very little about Holland or the outside world.

The frontier trekboers bred large and vigorous families while living in modest and probably temporary housing. They spent their lives in supervising their bondsmen herders and servants; hunting for meat, hides, and ivory was their recreation. They gained intellectual stimulation from the Dutch Calvinist Bible of their forefathers, usually Old Testament readings that comforted and justified them in their patriarchal outlook toward neighbors, strangers, and natives. These families broke their social isolation but a few times a year, for reunions in connection with religious rites (marriage, baptism, con-

A rural Boer family gathers for a daily Bible reading.

firmation). On their own, they were as fiercely self-reliant as they
needed to be: The company never troubled to provide effective
protection.

The frontier Boers relied upon tested military advantages, like
horseback rifle marksmanship, and the potential mobility of their
ox-drawn wagons as refuge and fortress. When faced by threat of
native attack, or the need to retaliate for thievery or murder, the
neighborhood "commando" would be rounded up by galloping messengers, and this local militia would ride out to exterminate the
marauding Bushmen, or out on the eastern frontier to gingerly harass
the Bantu, while recapturing stolen cattle and often taking along

A Boer instructs his son in the manly rite of the rifle.

many more from the native kraals. Sudden death was accepted as a part of their life-style, but their superior weaponry afforded a wide killing edge, especially against the outmatched Bushmen.

Sir John Barrow, traveling extensively in the South African back country near 1800, thought the Boers were dull and unlettered, but he wrote an affecting portrait of the breed:

> *The women of the African peasantry lead a life of the most listless inactivity. The mistress of the family, with her coffee-pot constantly boiling before her on a small table, seems fixed to her chair like a piece of the furniture; and it is the business*

of a little black boy or a Hottentot, wholly naked, to attend her with a small branch of a tree or a fan made of ostrich feathers to flap away the flies. . . . The young girls sit with their hands before them as listless as their mothers. Most of them, in the distant districts, can neither read nor write, so they have no mental resources whatsoever. Luckily, perhaps, for them, the paucity of ideas prevents time from hanging heavy on their hands. The history of a day is that of their whole lives. . . .

The young people have no meetings at fixed periods, as in most country places, for mirth and recreation. No fairs, no dancing, no music, nor amusement of any sort. To the cold phlegmatic temper and inactive way of life may perhaps be owing the prolific tendency of all the African peasantry. Six or seven children in a family are considered as very few; from a dozen to twenty are not uncommon; and most of them marry very young, so that the population of the country is rapidly increasing. . . .

The men are in general much above the middle size, very tall and stout, but ill made, loosely put together, awkward, and inactive. . . . Rude and uncultivated as are their minds, there is one virtue in which they eminently excel—hospitality to strangers. . . .

When a traveller arrives at a habitation, he alights from his horse, enters the house, shakes hands with the men, kisses the women, and sits down without further ceremony. When the table is served he takes his place among the family without waiting for an invitation. . . . If there is a bed in the house it is given to the stranger; if none . . . he must take his chance for a form, or bench, or a heap of sheep-skins, among the rest of the family. . . . In this manner a traveller might pass through the whole country.

Another traveler, George Thompson, held kindlier views on the Boers—"a shrewd, prudent, persevering, good-humoured, hospitable, and respectable class of men." Daniel Boone and Davy Crockett, trans-Appalachian pioneers alive at this time, would have endorsed the Boer boldness and assurance. The white's attitude toward the natives was the same on either frontier: When you see me coming, step aside!

This was the period the Bushmen were decimated. These people did not understand the principle of private ownership of livestock, and as their natural source of wild animals declined, they were pushed into greater thievery, and sometimes murder, usually of Hottentot herd boys. The resulting Dutch commando retaliations were massive and cruel.

Adriaan van Jaarsveld led a commando against a Bushmen area, but was unable to find the enemy in his thicketed hillside refuge. Van Jaarsveld then directed his unit to slaughter twelve hippopotamuses along a river course below. The militia withdrew into watchful ambush, and when the Bushmen came to the bait and were in the midst of feasting, the commando attacked, killing 122 and capturing 21. The Boer practice was to kill all adult males, and perhaps their women, too, to take surviving dependents, mainly children, and distribute them as slave laborers and servants. In this manner Bushman blood entered the mix of the Cape Coloured population.

George Thompson, the traveler, tells of a perceptive Boer who, realizing that Bushmen aggressions were often prompted by sheer hunger, kept a few goats to be driven to the Bushmen camp in bad times. This farmer found the kindness given back by the Bushmen, who protected his flocks. But this humane exchange was rare indeed. In 1792, the company offered a cash bounty for any Bushman captured; he was to be sent to a prison island for lifetime labor.

What of the Hottentots? They had been destroyed as a cohesive, self-governing people well before 1800. Their lack of Dutch-style ambition did them in economically; alcohol addiction was ruinous;

Boer expansion pushed them from their lands; and a terrible small-pox epidemic early on destabilized many tribal organizations. Eventually most of the true or part Hottentots became vagrants or laborers and servants of the whites.

Hottentot disinterest in work remained high, but with their natural talent for the job, they found work as herd boys out with the cattle. A Hottentot corps of soldiery was later recruited by the English; they were much admired and used against hereditary foes, Bushmen and Bantu. Like the Indian scouts assisting the United States Army on the frontier, their tracking skills were superb.

The free mixed-race offspring of whites and Hottentots were proud of their white blood in a demoralized native society, and tended to intermarry to preserve it. They proudly called themselves the Bastaards, and formed yet another strain in the South African racial mixture. The company law against Hottentot enslavement continued, but on the farm their lot was about the same as a slave's. Boers, taking their master race role seriously, were a law unto themselves in relations with their native servants, free or slave. Their Bible told them so.

The book of Genesis (chapter 9) reported the patriarch Noah cursing his son Ham and condemning his dark-skinned descendants to being bonded to other races. In the book of Joshua (chapter 9), the prophet encountered a tribe of Ham's descendents, who were, like the Hottentots of old, uncooperative to self-important visitors. After a suggestion that the culprits be slaughtered was kindly vetoed by the prophet, Joshua solemnly declared:

> *Now therefore ye are cursed, and there shall none of you be freed from being bondsmen, and hewers of wood and drawers of water for the house of my God.*

South African Boer patriarchs then, later, and still, enforce a narrow role for native Africans: common laborers maintaining the white's house.

Then into this Old Testament backwater came new strangers from overseas—the English—with a liberal philosophy toward the natives that shocked the Boers.

Turmoil in Holland caused by the French Revolution brought the English to occupy Capetown in 1795 to prevent a similar French conquest there. Next, in 1798, the war-battered Dutch East Indies Company ended in bankruptcy. In the Napoleonic Wars settlement, England received South Africa as a permanent colony, a strategic prize but little else. The country appeared to hold no wealth, just a population of stubborn Dutchmen.

When the new Cape Colony owners announced that English would be the official language, the Boers shook their heads; it would be impossible. The English were too few and stuck away in Capetown. When English missionaries then began ministering to the natives, the Boers were displeased. Believing in the Calvinist doctrine of predestination and that the destination for inferior heathen was hell, they thought religious indoctrination a waste. And they became jealous of the missionary attempts to rejuvenate the Hottentot morally so that he might be set on his own way economically. This smacked of tampering with the master/servant relationship! Then, when these upstart foreigners began to openly champion the servants' civil rights versus their masters', the masters were appalled and outraged.

The London Missionary Society, formed in 1795, the same year the English first came to South Africa, was a powerful global forerunner of the type of civil-rights organization that became prominent in the mid-twentieth century. It preached a social gospel, being at least as interested in the worldly condition of downtrodden races as in their immortal souls. The great objective of "The Philanthropists" in England was the end of slavery within the British Empire. William Wilberforce and associates achieved this in two steps: From 1807, no new slaves could be bought, and in 1833 slavery itself was abolished.

That this was accomplished illustrated a great deal of organized political might against powerful vested interests (many of the great private fortunes in England grew from profits of slavery). The society's missionaries in South Africa were not isolated idealists performing their civil uplift work among the natives. They wrote letters that wound up on important desks in the Colonial Office in London, the administrator of the Cape Colony. Prompted by Dr. John Philip and Thomas Pringle, superb traveling public relations conductors for the London Missionary Society, allies in the Colonial Office overrode as necessary the policies of the resident English governor in Capetown. For about thirty years the LMS had it both ways, at both ends.

In 1809 the natives were registered by residence and job and needed a pass to change either (pass laws remain a regulatory tool of apartheid). The registration was aimed at the numerous Hottentot vagrants, who were thereby halted in their wanderings and nudged toward taking service with a white. Since expansion of the institution of slavery was now forbidden, the Cape Colony benefited by this tightening of the labor supply. The act did take notice of the Hottentots as a class under the law, and the Boers grumbled suspiciously over this shadow of government supervision of *their servants.*

Then, in 1812, came the "Black Circuits," making a stinging departure into the new era. Two LMS activists, Dr. Van der Kemp and James Read, gathered pages of alleged abuses from their Hottentot followers and mailed the sensational material to London. The result was that the new traveling circuit court in the South African provinces received from the Colonial Office about sixty cases arraigning whites on charges by free blacks alleging cruelty or fraud. In several of the cases, the charge was murder!

Being compelled to defend themselves in a one-to-one situation opposite their servants was to most Boers an inconceivable concept that worked to destroy the time-sanctified authority of the master. Coerced into cooperation with the court, the defendants saw it as racial humiliation—and in public, too.

The English judges winnowed down the evidence and found some cause in only eight cases (no murders), and directed compensation.

The hearsay charges often evaporated: An old Boer housewife was accused of torturing a Hottentot by scalding him. In court it was brought out that the herd boy had become confused in an unexpected snowfall, was found semiconscious, brought in, and, during the woman's ministrations with hot water to revive the native, one of his feet was slightly burned.

The precedent set by the black circuits was, to the masters, terrible and demeaning; to the servants, it was attractive and available. Complaints increased in following years. Probably the threat of court inquiry caused proprietors to curb their tempers. But crowding the Boers was a dangerous game. There were half-wild, unreasonable individuals out there, as the local authorities—if not the London Missionary Society—understood.

Frederick Bezuidenhout was a tough farmer living on the dangerous Bantu frontier on the east. His Hottentot servant, Booy, ran away to the local authority, alleging cruelty. Ordered to personally appear, Bezuidenhout declined, but wrote a reasonable letter of explanation and countercharges. He diplomatically said he was too ill to travel. The dispute was "adjusted" and Booy returned. Twice more Booy departed and made complaints; twice more the farmer remained firm in refusing to come in, though again writing reasonable letters of explanation. All involved understood that the Boer was showing contempt for outside interference.

Finally, Booy, who had of free will signed a new contract with the farmer, left Bezuidenhout again. This time he lodged a claim for money and property, and joined the Hottentot dragoons army unit. The official order demanding satisfaction was carried by Booy to the police officer of Bezuidenhout's district. The officer was afraid of the Boer and sent Booy on alone. The farmer admittedly beat the Hottentot "until my stick was broken."

This series of events began in April 1813, dragging through to the beating in May 1815. Still, due process, and the unwillingness of the local authority to physically take on Frederick Bezuidenhout, delayed further action until October 1815. Wary officials then sent in a sufficient force, including black troopers. The defiant Bezuiden-hout had prepared a final stand in a cave that could not be approached except by one man at a time. After starting the shooting, he retreated there. After a long spell of shouting back and forth brought no result, a Hottentot sergeant, Joseph, volunteered to climb alone to the cave mouth. He began a conversation with the partially obscured Boer, but when onlookers shouted urgent warnings to Joseph, he fired, killing Bezuidenhout.

A Hottentot had killed a Boer with government permission! The shock wave ripped through the region. At the well-attended funeral, the deceased's brother, Johannes, proclaimed rebellion: They would drive the profane English and their Hottentot lackeys back over the mountains! But getting "they" together was slow; only a handful of hotheads responded. Then the rebels thought to tap a mighty ally. Messengers were sent to Gaika, great chief of the nearby Xhosa Bantus, offering generous territorial concessions in return for his warriors' aid.

Without waiting for a reply, Johannes Bezuidenhout then whip-sawed the settlers: Be for us, or you are against us; when Gaika comes, if you are not with us, you will be killed along with the English! By threat and exhortation, a force of about sixty men was collected. Meanwhile, government police and English army officers gathered a larger but modest force of loyal burghers and Hottentot dragoons and moved out seeking the rebels.

On November 18, 1815, the Bezuidenhout faction, deployed on high ground beside a pass called Slagter's Nek, was approached by the government force, and a tense standoff began. Colonel Jacob Cuyler of the government was determined to quash the insurrection there, by parley or by force. At this critical point the messengers returning from the Bantu meeting galloped into camp and told the rebel leaders that Gaika had absolutely refused to help, remarking he thought the colonists crazy, and that he had no intention of becoming "a silly deer between a lion on one side and a wolf on the other."

The rebels parleyed then with Cuyler, even after their impassioned request that black troopers be sent away was denied. Their militia surrendered, except Johannes Bezuidenhout and a few desperate companions. They fled, gathered their families and wagons, and made for the Bantu lands outside the Cape Colony.

The next day they were intercepted by a Hottentot unit officered by an Englishman. While the others surrendered or were captured, at the last it was Bezuidenhout with his wife and teenage son alone. Though tightly surrounded, he opened fire, killing a soldier. Return Hottentot fire into the wagon became intense as his wife, Martha, helped by reloading and occasionally firing herself, till all three were hit repeatedly and Johannes died. Martha afterward scorned medical aid from the English officer and managed to survive.

The two violent malcontents were dead, and by tempered imprisonments, banishments, fines—of which plenty were distributed—there should have been an end to it. But the English governor, Lord Charles Somerset, wanted to set a harsh example. Of the six death penalties sent up by the court for his review (and for expected clemency, as had been granted in past minor uprisings), the governor confirmed five sentences of death.

The grotesque outcome was the erection of a long gallows in the midst of a desert plain, in view of Slagter's Nek, with the ordered presence of every one-time rebel to witness the hanging of five of their friends, close associates of Johannes Bezuidenhout. Colonel Cuyler was present, bringing a security force of three hundred. A crowd of grieving or morbidly curious folk also stood by.

March 9, 1816: Slagter's Nek was a scene of utter desolation, human and physical. The wind whined over the scrubby expanse, whipping up clouds of dust. The convicts, having sung a last hymn, stood noosed on the platform, their homespun clothing fluttering in the gale, as Colonel Cuyler read their sentences. At length the signal was given, the five traps were sprung—and four of the five plunged through to the ground!

They sprang up, were joined by hysterical onlookers, and pleaded with the commander for mercy. But Cuyler had his orders and sustained a stolid discipline against their entreaties. All were re-hanged in emotional scenes of the cruelest character.

In an explanatory letter to higher authority, Colonel Cuyler reported that the hangman, coming from afar and having been misinformed, brought only one rope. No resident would sell or provide rope, the officer noted, but he found some stored in a government building, which proved rotten.

The intent of Lord Somerset—to abort future uprisings—was successful. But Slagter's Nek became a hateful symbol to the Boers of their bondage to unfeeling strangers. As recently as the 1960s, at least, the lonely monument marking the tragedy site and burial had been adorned with fresh flowers.

4

Shaka Zulu
and the Bantu Holocaust

The 1800s opened upon an impending racial collision on the Cape Colony's eastern frontier. Expansion overland had been normal and necessary for both the Boer and Bantu cattle-raising cultures. The white stock farmers preferred migration to the rainier east, rather than to the semidesert north, because pasturage improved in that direction.

But about seven hundred miles east of Capetown, the pioneers encountered the Xhosa tribe. This impressive western vanguard of the Bantu host was slowly expanding because of population pressures. Both races paused in a wavering standoff in the vicinity of the Great Fish River, which, despite its name, held little water and few fish. This easily fordable stream became the approximate black/white boundary in the century between 1750 and 1850.

The Dutch had handled the Hottentots and Bushmen to suit themselves. But the new black group they faced in the east was daunting in the size of its population alone. There were more than a million Bantu behind the Xhosa edge. Since the entire white Cape Colony population was below fifty thousand, it was lucky for the colonists that the Bantu mass did not then present the disciplined force that it would in the future.

The Bantu people were not predominantly warriors, and the half-dozen or so major Bantu tribal nations were not unified politically.

44

The whites were long in coming to understand this. A treaty with a "great chief" like Gaika did not aid dealing with other branches of the Xhosa Bantu.

Bantu social law allowed malcontents to migrate freely and to form new clans. So the personality and practices of the chiefs mattered. The Bantu manner of royal succession also encouraged tribal division. In this polygamous society, the chief produced sons from early wives, but usually added a "great wife" at the summit of his career, whose son he chose to be heir apparent. The elder sons, if ambitious, might intrigue against the heir or go off with a group of followers and begin a new tribal unit.

Clashes, rather than wars, between clans and tribes were nearly continuous. The universal pastime of cattle rustling provided the occasions; retaliation was a kind of national sport, often as prearranged tribal battles with their own cheering sections. Each fine-bodied six-foot warrior carried a tall, oval cattle-hide shield on an armband as protection, with a supply of four or five thin, light, six-foot iron-tipped spears called "assegais" (from the hard, native wood in the shafts). These were hurled with fair accuracy to fifty yards or more. The warrior retained one stabbing assegai for occasional close-in work. If often defeated, tribal units might move outward into the land that seemed as limitless to them as it did to the Boers.

Bantu men took care of their stock, while women tended to agriculture. Cattle were the means and currency of the Bantu good life. Each cattleman doted on his cows as individuals and delighted in having his wealth on the hoof paraded before him. His life ambition was to obtain more.

In this society, the strong-armed hero was admired, so youth was the time of preparation for and competition in image-building. The chiefs lived dangerously, vying in treacherous political dealings. They also spent much time in tribal judgment. Penalties for wrongdoing were either fines or a death sentence. The Bantu thought the white's use of prisons a barbarous cruelty.

The white's term for this populous race of blacks was Kaffirs (heathen), borrowed from the Arabic slang of East Coast slave traders. In later South African times, "kaffir" has become a put-down word for nonwhites, but it used to mean a worthy Bantu opponent, whether on the battlefield or in cattle thievery. There were nine Kaffir Wars on the eastern frontier between 1779 and 1877. The whites eventually won each of them, but several of the victories didn't result in any boundary shifts, so they didn't really gain the settlers very much.

As an example, the Fourth Kaffir War of 1811 occurred because of the unruly presence of about twenty thousand Xhosa in the Zuurveld, a prime grazing area on the English side of the Fish River. They were trespassers. After the previous war, the Xhosa chief Gaika had treatied to stay east of the stream, but another powerful Xhosa chief, Ndlambe, acted otherwise. Boer commandos and English and Hottentot troops harried the Bantu back across the river. A chain of block forts was installed along the river, and a military base established at Grahamstown.

But the countryside was too brushy, the patrol troops too few, and normal conditions returned. That is, raiding in both directions resumed. Boers lived illegally beyond the Fish, and Bantu rustlers roamed into the colony at will. The white's stock was easier to steal because it was often grazed in the open country. But though few in number, the Boer on horseback spoke with the long, accurate range of his rifle and, when riding in commando, the Boers were the more successful rustlers. White annals of the time dwell on the shifting fortunes—so many hundred or thousand cows stolen by the blacks, and so many more thousand stolen back in white commando raids.

In 1818, a witch doctor who had risen to power, Makana, stirred up the feud between chiefs Ndlamba and Gaika, and the bloody warfare that broke out resulted in Gaika's stinging defeat. He ran to the English, who supported him with a deep raid over the river. Chief Ndlambe had not expected white intervention in Xhosa affairs and, prompted by Makana, prepared vengeance. In April 1819, about ten thousand warriors, hopped up by Makana's promises of supernatural immunity, crossed the Fish and overran the Zuurveld, pillaging and killing among the isolated Boer homesteads (though always sparing women).

On the morning of April 22, three columns of thousands of Xhosa warriors attacked the redcoats defending unfortified Grahamstown. The English firing line discipline was precise. Just at the moment the Bantu host paused and drew back their arms to hurl a shower of assegais, one hundred muskets crashed in unison, battering and blunting the enemy front ranks. The blacks quickly reformed to attack again, but just as swiftly the redcoats reloaded and refired accurately. They were assisted by Hottentot sharpshooters skilled in recognizing and picking off warrior leaders. One penetration to the edge of the barracks area was beaten back by the black African Rifles unit. By sundown the warriors from across the river were long gone, leaving behind at least seven hundred dead. Redcoat casualties for the day were three killed and five wounded.

The instigator, Makana, was afterward chased down and sent to the government prison on Robben Island. He soon attempted escape but drowned in the attempt. Word of the event reached the Bantu lands. Since Makana was a powerful witch doctor, the Xhosa, for a long time, looked for his magical reappearance.

It had been a near disaster at Grahamstown, avoided by discipline, tactics, and good luck. So the British Colonial Office decided to fill the frontier with English settlers. A terrible, starving, postwar economic depression had settled over Britain. Those who could afford it were fleeing over the ocean to Canada and America, as many as two hundred a week. The British government advertised for four thousand settlers, offering free passage to South Africa, plus a small farm in the rural paradise of the Zuurveld. By reply it received ninety thousand applications and was able to select a group of English settlers to shore up the frontier, and, it was hoped, to begin dissolving the predominance of Boer culture.

The settlers sailed in twenty-one ships from various ports in the British Isles during the bleak English winter. They were favored with calm three-month voyages southward, arriving between April and June 1820, as the chilly South African winter set in. The debarkation at Algoa Bay (Port Elizabeth) was a colorful introduction to their primitive future ashore. The immigrants were carried through the cold surf on the backs of "yellow-faced Hottentots with pepper-corned hair," then were met by the Boer wagoneers, burly non–English speakers clad in picturesque leather and homespun with broad-brimmed hats, who had been hired to haul each family to its appointed homestead in the bush.

That wilderness trek took up several days, often more than a week. At journey's end, the agricultural tools and personal belongings were off-loaded, and after a rough handshake and a farewell in the Afri-kaner-Dutch dialect, the wagon creaked off and left the settler fam-ily alone upon its hundred acres in the backlands of the Zuurveld. Each day thereafter, the new farmers would remember Colonel Cuyler's strongest admonition at the settler briefings: "Gentlemen, when you go out to plough, never leave your guns at home."

The new pioneers gained memories of sights and sounds never forgotten. The Reverend Henry Dugmore reminisced:

Elephants in hundreds roamed leisurely from the Kooms to the Kowie. . . . The rhinoceros crushed at will the thickets of the Fish River ravines. The lion stalked in undisputed sover-eignty on the slopes of the Winterberg and his roar was occasionally heard in the lower districts. The howl and laugh of the hyena, and the shrill yell of the jackal were regular nightly serenade of the new settlers to which the little ones listened and trembled.

Over half of the settlers had emigrated from Britain's depressed cities and had no farming skills. In any case, the first three crops were destroyed by plant disease and drought. The newcomers required welfare assistance to stave off hunger. It was not until the later introduction of a wool industry from imported Merino sheep that there was much prosperity in the Albany (Zuurveld) district.

In these conditions, many settlers abandoned rural pursuits and retreated to more familiar grounds of Port Elizabeth, Capetown, and the few other cities. They became skilled artisans and opened businesses, thereby establishing an occupational separation of the two white groups, as well as a language separation. The English in South Africa tended to follow urban careers, while the Boers, as before, dominated the countryside.

Meanwhile, new problems were developing on the eastern frontier. At the close of the 1818 war, the blacks had been driven across the Keiskamma River, and the strip from there to the Fish River had been declared an empty buffer zone. Without contact, peace would be assured between black and white adversaries. However, the thrifty British Colonial Office again pared away the troops who might have policed the zone. Soon Boer and Bantu were back to quarreling.

But far to the east, in the unknown Bantu interior, an extreme political and military upheaval, which involved and destroyed many Bantu tribal structures, took place behind the Xhosa domains in the region called Natal. The terrible life and times of Shaka Zulu radically altered the story of South African history.

The Nguni branch of the Bantu peoples in 1800 filled an attractive grazing and agricultural area stretching eastward for hundreds of miles from the Xhosa frontier near the Fish River. A formidable mountain range that the whites would call Drakensberg raised a natural northern boundary, and the lowland jungles of Portuguese Mozambique to the east and the southern ocean otherwise enclosed Natal.

Near its center lived a small tribe, the Zulu, who were destined to rise from insignificance, on the verge of incredible expansion and conquest. Shaka, their military leader, was alive in 1800 as a socially insecure herd boy. The story of the rise of the Zulu nation begins with another warrior of local renown—Dingiswayo.

He began as Godongwana, an elder son of Chief Jobe of the

medium-size Umtetwa tribe. In familiar Bantu royal treachery, he and a brother plotted, or were suspected of planning, to murder their father, who had picked a young son as ruling heir. But Chief Jobe struck first. In the night a hit squad killed one elder son, but Godong-wana ran into the dark bush with an assegai blade stuck between his shoulders. He recovered and became a fugitive prince with a price on his head. Traveling long and hard, he renamed himself Dingis-wayo (Distressed Wanderer) and was finally taken in far to the north by a chief, Bungane, not friendly to his father.

Then in 1806 or 1807, the strangest creature ever seen by the interior Bantu rode south through a pass in the Drakensberg. It was an *umlungu* (white devil)!

> *. . . a marvel; his garment though so small as to be held in the grasp of his hand, when slipped over his head, covered his body; his hat, which he removed at pleasure, was conceived to be part of his head; his shoes made it appear that he was devoid of toes, and . . . his heel was so long as to penetrate the ground.*

> *He was mounted on an animal of great speed, and carried a pole in his hands which spat fire and thunder, and killed all wild animals he looked at. . . .*

> *At his presence the natives fled, after killing an ox to be consumed by him, and whenever he entered a kraal beads and brass and other trinkets were left behind where he had been sitting.*

It was supposed that he was a great foreign witch doctor. And indeed Chief Bungane, who, braver than the others, invited him to stop at his kraal, had a troublesome knee operated on and healed by the white wizard. He was probably Dr. Robert Cowan, a military surgeon and member of a small expedition seeking an overland route

Shaka Zulu, from Nathaniel Isaac's Travels and Adventures in Eastern Africa *(1836).*

from the Cape Colony to Mozambique, who marched into the eastern wilderness in 1806 and vanished.

The stranger desired an escort to guide him southward to the sea, three hundred miles away. Dingiswayo agreed or was coerced into going along, and thus spent some possibly fruitful weeks in the doctor's company. Eventually, they entered the last jurisdiction near the seacoast, that of Chief Phakathwayo of the Qwabe tribe. They had fanciful ideas of the white men:

> *A belief was prevalent . . . that white men were not human beings but a production of the sea, which they traversed in large shells, coming near the shores in stormy weather, their food being the tusks of elephants, which they would take from the beach if laid there for them, and placing beads in their room, which they obtained from the bottom of the sea.*

Unable to bear having such an unnatural being present among his tribe, Chief Phakathwayo had the white monster killed. Dingiswayo, whether bystander or participant, inherited the magic of the horse and gun.

Thus equipped, the long-distressed wanderer hastened to the fringes of his Umtetwa homeland and, displaying his potent magic, soon gathered a force that drove his younger brother from the throne. The new chief announced that though Chief Jobe in life hated him as Godongwana, now in death his spirit favored him as Dingiswayo.

A native genius at military statecraft, Dingiswayo organized his army into a disciplined force where command and promotion were based on merit. Because of similarities to European organization, it is believed by some authorities that he was a quick study in listening to Dr. Cowan, or in observing the Portuguese soldiers, who for the sake of the ivory trade assisted him in his first war, against that same Chief Phakathwayo, who made the mistake of shielding Dingiswayo's deposed brother.

Leading disciplined, coordinated forces, Dingiswayo won every tribal war in the vicinity. But he did not round up the enemy's cattle and just go home again. Instead, the defeated tribe or clan was taken over and placed under a puppet chief. Perhaps this potent new approach was suggested by the pressures of increasing population. The losers kept their cattle, but provided warriors for their own regiment in the winner's army. Dingiswayo thus assembled an empire and added military muscle with every tribal conquest.

One of the small tribes added later was the Zulu, whose chief, Zenzangakona, surrendered before battle and kept his throne. This chief, as a teenager in about 1787, had fathered an illegitimate child. When word came from the girl's Lengani clan that Nandi was pregnant, Zenzangakona's family tried a royal cover-up. They decreed that she suffered from the *I-shaka,* an intestinal parasite that bloated her abdomen. They sent her back. Afterward Nandi returned to the Zulu with her infant son, who had been sarcastically named Shaka (parasite).

The parents married, but split when the boy was about six years old. Nandi was too willful and unsparing of her husband's royal prerogatives, so Zenzangakona banished his bad-tempered wife and unwanted son. Shaka's childhood was transient and insecure, and he absorbed much scorn, especially in the years that he spent in the kraals of his mother's tribe. But, he became a superb physical specimen, half a head taller than his competitors and detractors; and then he joined Dingiswayo's army.

Since that army rewarded merit and bravery, Shaka, excelling at both, swiftly rose to become a regimental commander and later a confidante of Dingiswayo. As a result, in 1816, after the natural death of his father, Shaka became chief of the Zulus, with Dingiswayo's approval, by arranging the murder of his younger half-brother royal heir. Chief Shaka Zulu, beyond being an inspiring battle leader, was a bold innovator in military weapons and tactics.

For example, he scorned the slim, thrown assegais. Shaka had a heavy, true-stabbing assegai crafted, one called *ixwa,* after the sucking sound the thick blade made when being withdrawn from an opponent's abdomen. It was the sole weapon his warriors carried. Shaka also designed a hooking edge to the great Zulu shields, which, catching an opponent's shield, twisted him off balance and opened him to the thrust of the *ixwa*. Always leading the charge, in these early days, was Shaka, who would bellow *Ngadla!* (I have eaten!) after each personal kill.

Zulu blacksmiths smelt iron ore and shape ixwas.

The attack unit *(impi)* was redesigned by Shaka. About two-thirds of the body would charge in a standard, but now disciplined, rush. Just before contact with the braced, compact mass of foes though, a group of warriors would scoot out to either side of Shaka's *impi* to enclose the distraught enemy's flanks. Meanwhile, the one-third in reserve could be commanded into the fight at the most needed, or advantageous, spot. "Head, horns, chest" became the standard Zulu attack tactic for decades.

This tactic required speed, and Shaka was prepared. Long ago, as a warrior, he had kicked off sandals and toughened his bare feet. After becoming chief, he ordered his soldiers to do the same. They were rather slow about it, for Natal was a thorny countryside. But Shaka would not be thwarted.

He scheduled a regimental dance and had the field thickly sown in thorns. In the beginning Shaka danced gracefully, smilingly, alone on the thorn-strewn ground. He ordered his warriors to join him barefooted and then retired to watch. The troops were far from enthusiastic dancers. They lurched about grotesquely, oohing and ouching. A movement started to hobble off the field.

Grim Chief Shaka and a hit squad met these individuals, who were killed on the spot. After a dozen or so casualties, the dancers got the point(s). They pranced on in relative silence, joined again by tough-heeled Shaka. Together they danced—it seemed an agonizing hour—as blood spurted and strangled grunts were heard, but the thorn stomp went on!

Beyond valor and military ingenuity, death was the terrible command tactic of Shaka. He was *ruthless*—ruthless far beyond any of his contemporaries in the Bantu lands. He showed it in his first battle under the gaze of Dingiswayo.

It was a small tribal fight with the Butelezi. They proposed single combat, and Shaka came out to oppose the Butelezi champion. The latter hurled assegais, which Shaka deflected with his shield as he unexpectedly charged, came up and hooked aside his opponent's shield, spearing the warrior with the *ixwa: Ngadla!*

The Butelezi supposed the encounter was over, but Shaka charged on toward the main body alone, followed by the mass of his fleet *impi*. In terror, the defenders flung down their shields (indicating surrender) and fled. But Shaka had only begun. The fleeing warriors were cut down, and Shaka and company had reached the sanctuary of women and children with clear intent to massacre, when Dingiswayo called a halt.

In the two years after Shaka became the Zulu chieftan and before his betrayal of Dingiswayo, he was unable to convince the senior leader of the wisdom of wiping out whole tribes, so that they could never be a problem again. Perhaps this disagreement hurried Shaka into treachery.

Dingiswayo prepared for war against the threat of Zwide, a powerful tribal confederationist himself, in the north of Natal. Shaka was enlisted to lead half of the army in a pincer attack on Zwide. Tradition has it that Shaka betrayed his partner's location to Zwide; or that Shaka delayed his side of the pincer attack. Dingiswayo was captured and executed. His skull joined a rack of other chiefs' skulls in the witch hut of Zwide's mother.

Shaka maneuvered himself into Dingiswayo's place. Life went forward differently under him: terrible abroad, frightening at home. Shaka slaughtered tribes: men, women, children, wherever his *impis* could reach them. Sometimes teenagers, young men, were spared to be bound into the Zulu army. Eventually even mighty Zwide's confederation was destroyed, his old witch mother placed in a cage with a hyena, who, by small bites, killed her slowly.

Knowing their certain fate, tribes small and large panicked and fled, blundering and killing through other tribal homelands across hundreds of miles before resettling. These included some from Dingiswayo's confederation, for with Shaka, no other tribe could coexist. Become Zulu or be dead!

Starvation, causing cannibalism, was rampant in the broad scorched-earth "traffic deserts" that encircled Shaka's Zulu homeland. Bantu southern Africa all the way up to the Zambezi River rocked in shock waves of people fleeing Shaka's kraal, Bulawayo (the killing place), in south-central Natal. The human debris has been estimated at over a million dead, as Shaka annihilated about ninety tribes and clans and boosted his Zulu nation from (estimates) 2,000 to 250,000—in five to eight years! That was the Bantu holocaust.

This record is hearsay, for by the time that the first whites met Shaka in 1824, the conquering phase of the Zulu empire was past, there being no more Bantu tribes handy to kill. Henry Francis Fynn, a literate young Englishman, is the source of nearly all that has been told here, beginning with the *umlungu,* Dr. Cowan. In parts of four years at the Zulu court as Shaka's white confidant, the adventurous young man learned the language and recorded the recent traditional history of the Zulu nation.

The fortunate Fynn, at twenty-one a member of a venturesome trading expedition exploring in 1824 the edges of European settlement, was walking along a Natal beach pondering the rumor of Shaka Zulu and how he might be contacted, when he was startled by the thumping of thousands of bare feet on sand and saw a vast column of Zulu soldiers coming up the beach at a trot. The *indunas* (leaders) were as amazed as he, but, luckily, signed neutrality. The bemused Fynn watched about twenty thousand warriors pass in jogging procession. Surely there was something to the stories of a Bantu superking!

Shaka knew vaguely of white men and their articles of magic. Dingiswayo had related his experiences; also, there was at the Zulu court a well-traveled Xhosa who had spent time with the whites (in jail for cattle rustling). But, strangers on his coast were few, and the savage king thought them no threat. It would be diverting to observe them, to display the Zulu splendor. And when the royal summons came, Fynn and two senior companions eagerly agreed to the remarkable risk of going inland to Shaka's kraal, because as traders they craved his ivory and his permission to establish a trading station.

En route to the monarch's court, Fynn, who had received preliminary medical training in London before following his family to South Africa, treated an ailing native woman. Rumor enlarged this act into raising her from the dead. Naturally, Shaka was curious; after leading a show-off dancing marathon and military and cattle parades involving most of the estimated eighty thousand Zulu present, Shaka, then about thirty-seven years of age, ordered the Xhosa renegade he kept at court to interpret for an interview testing young Fynn's witchdoctor abilities. At the end of the interview he invited the young man to stay on.

Shaka always spoke of his subjects degradingly. He called them his dogs. What was a "dog's" life for the ordinary man?

Unfortunately, superstition had raised the cult of the witch doctors to terrifying prominence. Zulu-watcher Henry Fynn paused in a village to observe a witch doctor at his practice.

> Our attention was drawn to a party of 150 natives sitting in a circle with a man opposite them, apparently interrogating them. In reply, they each beat the ground with a stick and said Yizwa Zhi! probably "Agreed!" After they had been answering with the same words about an hour, three of them were pointed out and killed on the spot. This man, whom they called an inyanga . . . was dressed in an ape skin cap; a number of pieces of different roots were tied round his neck; and a small shield and an assegai were in one hand, and the tail of a cow in the other. He was an interpreter of dreams and thought capable of telling what has happened in any other part of the country, also if one has injured another by poison or otherwise. His decision is fatal to the unfortunate individuals pointed out by him.

The belief of the Bantu in the ability of the witch doctor to "smell out" criminal intent, or the lurking presence of evil within a person, was so total that even the victim, if he or she knew of the sentence before time, believed the witch doctor and submitted passively to their death.

It was the mind-binding inspiration of Shaka Zulu to organize his nation's witch doctors to terrorize the people into submission. At Shaka's court Fynn saw that:

No sooner is the signal given, and the object pointed out, than those sitting round him scramble to kill him, although they have good reason to expect the next moment the same fate themselves, but such apprehensions are far from their thoughts; the will of the King being uppermost.

Atrocity was banal at Shaka's court; Fynn reports: "On one occasion I witnessed 60 boys under 12 years of age dispatched before he breakfasted." These may have been herd boys accused (convicted) of drinking milk from the royal herd, who, sentenced by the witch doctors, dutifully trudged to the executioners, reported their sentence, and were killed.

Being a warrior hero far away on the battlefronts was no insurance. It was necessary to fling oneself with utter reckless fury on the enemy, because after each engagement the *impi* commander selected his cowards and delivered them to Shaka's hit squads. And if there were no slackers, only heroes? The minimum quota was likely still delivered!

Shaka seems to have been one of the great woman haters of history. He never married, saying he scorned producing offspring who might one day kill him. He kept his army in bachelor status, too, only grudgingly allowing them to marry toward middle age and after supreme valor. Fynn reports the tyrant kept a harem of up to five thousand.

Shaka, according to Fynn, was very touchy on the subject of fatherhood, too:

Nandi, his mother, governed his concubines. She produced an infant with its mother to Shaka, observing that, from the likeness she could trace in the child, it was his. . . . He immediately seized the little innocent, and, throwing it up into the air, it was killed by the fall; the mother was instantly ordered to be put to death, whilst Shaka so severely beat his mother, Nandi, with a stick, for presuming to accuse him of being the father, that she was lame for three months.

But when, in 1827, his mother died, Shaka was greatly saddened. Knowing this, and also believing that undetected evildoers in the community must have caused Nandi's death, the lookout was on for the dry-eyed and unhysterical. These were ferociously attacked and murdered by the true mourners. Eyewitness Fynn thought that about seven thousand persons perished in this maelstrom of crazy vengeance, some by sheer exhaustion from excessive mourning. When the "great female elephant" was buried, ten of her servants, legs and arms broken but still somewhat alive, were entombed with Nandi.

Perhaps the impetus of Shaka's terror-supported reign expended itself amid this season of prolonged mourning, for in the following year, 1828, in the longstanding fashion of Bantu treachery, Shaka was stabbed to death by two half-brothers. His regiments cheered when they heard the news. The body was stuffed into an unused grain pit, its exact location unmarked and forgotten.

5

Over the Hills and Far Away

The murderous attacks of Shaka's Zulu *impis* led to related slaughters committed upon other native peoples by strong tribes carving out new homelands after fleeing from the approaching Zulus. The depopulation caused a vacuum across great stretches of the high veld north and east of the Cape Colony borders. Aware of this opportunity, some frontier Boers, dissatisfied with the English rule, decided to fill that vacuum themselves.

Since Slagter's Nek, the Boer list of grievances had expanded beyond the tolerance of many of their patriarchs. In a land where Dutch-Afrikaans had been the native tongue for hundreds of years, English had now been appointed the sole legal language. And in the touchy area of religion, the English were placing Scottish clergy in the Dutch Reformed Church! Meanwhile, the liberal missionary attempt to do away with the Boer master-and-servant relationship triumphed with the passage of Ordinance 50 in 1828.

This "Magna Charta of the natives" stated that "all Hottentots or other free persons of colour, lawfully residing in the colony, are in the most full and ample manner entitled to all and every right, benefit, and privilege to which any other British subjects are entitled." Well, many Hottentots exercised their right in the most full and ample manner of not working! They returned from holiday only

61

A freed slave jubilantly carries home the proclamation.

as necessity drove them, and found they could now bargain for wages and working conditions, as their Boer employers frowned.

More turmoil in the labor market was just ahead. In 1834 slavery was abolished in the British Empire, though four years were allowed for the social adjustments the statute demanded. The compensation that slave owners sought from the government was whittled in half, and then could only be obtained by paperwork done in London. The necessity of South Africans hiring go-between agents further reduced their payment.

Most importantly, the Boers were running out of land within the colony, and the eastern border had for long been stalled on the Fish River. British Colonial Office policy was not to enclose the Bantu and create new native problems. Neither would the officials expend the money and military buildup necessary to drive the Xhosa tribe permanently eastward to open new lands for their colonists. Then, the government in Capetown announced that the loan farm arrangement was ending. There would be land auctions; stockmen would have to pay and become true landowners, with taxes sure to follow. The almost-free ride on the open range was over.

Meanwhile, the restless stock farmers had learned a great deal about the forbidden territory from far-ranging hunters and ivory collectors. The word had been widely passed that much of that veld across the river was lush and well-watered, a grazing paradise teeming with wild meat available for Boer pots. It was a better land than their present holdings and, since the Bantu wars, attractively empty. The grass was definitely greener on the other side.

The British Colonial Office, influenced by the visionary Dr. Philip and the London Missionary Society, was determined to keep the white population in place, and the adjacent native tribal lands free of Boer social corruption. Dr. Philip dreamed of Christianizing and civilizing the neighboring native potentates and kingdoms by placing LMS missionaries at the chiefs' right hands. Black Africa for black Africans, morally uplifted, was the English theme of the 1830s.

The Boers disliked the language and native rights laws the English had laid on them; now, economically, they looked forward with great expectations, for, once settled on the high veld, they could forget the British and govern themselves and their servants in a new pastoral paradise, and according to Old Testament theories of race.

Piet Retief and Gert Maritz were two frontier personalities who organized their countrymen to prepare for the "Great Trek," which

over several years moved more than twelve thousand Boers into new
lands away from English control. Methodically, in 1834, three exploration parties scouted northwest, northeast, and east. If the British
knew at all, they thought these were hunting expeditions—for ivory,
not land.

The northwest report was negative; only the Kalahari Desert lay
that way. The northeast explorers found high, grassy, empty veld
northward, but cautioned of the warrior (ex-Zulu) Matabele tribe
based in the distant north near the Limpopo River. Future trek
leader Piet Uys's party probed due east through the Xhosa and
Mponda tribal lands and discovered the lush, empty swath of Natal
that was the Zulu buffer zone.

Uys was so impressed with Natal's potential that he gave way to
assumptions that would be fatal to himself and others later on.
Unable to reach the present Zulu despot, Dingane, he allowed
himself to believe, from a shouted conversation across a flooded
stream with a Zulu *induna,* that the Boers would be welcomed in
filling out a buffer state beside the Zulus. Uys's tribal bargainings
were naïve generally; a Mponda chief gave Uys land belonging to the
rival Xhosa tribe, and a Xhosa chieftan in his turn offered a strip of
Mponda territory!

Piet Retief, on the basis of Uys's glowing report, resolved to make
a future voortrek to Natal.

The first trekker, however, to turn away from the Cape Colony
for good was Boer patriarch Louis Tregardt, who plotted a northward route. Already living across the border in Xhosa tribal lands,
he was wanted, wrongly, by Cape authorities as the instigator in the
outbreak of another border war that started in December 1834.

Leading several families, Tregardt in early 1835 crossed the Orange River and moved northeast through uninhabited veld to the
next major river, the Vaal, and boldly across, all the way to the edge
of the lowlands along the Limpopo River, which remains a modern
boundary of the Republic of South Africa. Tregardt's trekkers settled peaceably in a beautiful upland area they called Zoutpansberg
to await the arrival of Boer brethren they believed would follow

along their wagon tracks. This self-reliant group had penetrated about seven hundred miles beyond the colony border.

At the same time, another group had independently set off on the same course, becoming for a time fellow travelers with Tregardt's people. Johannes Van Rensburg, the other trekker, did not get on well with Louis Tregardt. After being criticized by Tregardt for wasting gunpowder, the Van Rensburgs veered eastward, disappearing over the horizon and out of life. Eventually a Tregardt scouting party searched and found the site where the entire Van Rensburg group, families totaling about forty persons, had been slaughtered in a native attack. They had placed their wagons in the standard Boer laager, a defensive position: The wagons were parked in an interlocking square or circle with oxen and horses inside. In Van Rensburg's case this had probably been effective until he ran out of gunpowder.

During the next few years, the frequent passage of voortrekkers furrowed the veld in a broad band of wagon ruts that groups or individuals could follow like a freeway.

A typical trekking family owned a sturdy covered wagon, or wagons, each drawn by teams of twelve or sixteen oxen. The wagon boxes were high-sided and narrow: three-by-fourteen feet in surface area, built to carry about twenty-four hundred pounds apiece. Perhaps three hundred pounds of gunpowder, the most irreplaceable store, was carried. Portable household goods, a feather mattress, tools, a plow, roots of grapevines and fruit trees, and even a roost place for barnyard fowl, filled out the wagons.

Hottentot or Bushman servants drove or led the oxen and also attended to the accompanying family cattle, sheep, and goats. The men of the family ranged about the herds on horseback and hunted meat for the evening pot. The trek moved very slowly, at the pace of its animals. Speed didn't matter. Their faith in carrying out God's will for them matched their self-sufficiency: The men directed and hunted; the women organized and crafted; and the children helped. This practical arrangement kept a trekking family going on its own for months, or even a year, as necessary.

The next trek of major importance was carried out by Hendrik Potgieter and Sarel Cilliers with a merged group of about sixty-five families. Cilliers contented himself with being the trekker's spiritual leader and deferred to Potgieter in practical affairs. Potgieter, a bulky commanding figure standing six foot three, was the stiffest and sternest of all the trek leaders.

These emigrants departed the colony in late 1835, moving up about halfway between the Orange and Vaal rivers to stay awhile at the missionary outpost of Thaba Nchu, the kraal of Chief Moroka of the medium-size Seluka tribe. This lesser chief, fearing the return of marauding Zulu or Matabele *impis*, welcomed the protective presence of the whites, and held them by offering excellent pasturing on an open-ended basis. In this way Thaba Nchu became the trek meeting place of the future.

Potgieter and Cilliers then moved slowly northward, preparing to settle, making land contracts with the few tribes remaining from the Bantu holocaust. Families began to leave the main group at a point on the Sand River near the Vaal. Potgieter organized a small scouting commando, including Cilliers, to follow Tregardt's track. The isolated Boers were glad to see their brethren, for their supplies were dwindling. They were gratified when Potgieter agreed to come up with his followers and join the settlement of the attractive Zoutpansberg area, and also promised to resupply Tregardt. But when the commando returned south, they discovered the Matabele had recently attacked outlying families at Sand River and would surely return.

The Matabele tribe was the creation of Mzilikazi, a chief lieutenant of Shaka in his Zulu wars of extermination. Mzilikazi, after sharp disagreement with the Zulu king, fled with his considerable following, sweeping northwestward and smashing the Bantu kraals in his path. They did not halt until they were well north of the Vaal River. There they organized into the Matabele nation. Having held off vengeful expeditions sent after them from Zululand—and now twenty thousand warriors strong—they feared no man. Their important kraal at Mosega lay only about 150 miles from the Sand River

Boers. So Mzilikazi sent down a small *impi,* just a raiding party of six hundred warriors to wipe them out.

The trekboers, preferring isolation except in emergencies, had strung out in the area with distances of a few miles between family wagon settlements. Two parties had located beyond the Vaal and were closest to the striking point of the Matabele. Twenty-four emigrants were butchered in the Liebenberg camp, but the Botha and Steyn families got their wagons into laager and, mustering thirty guns, held off the attack, killing about one hundred fifty Matabele while losing only one man. In both attacks, the warriors drove off the Boers' cattle. But, out of the Liebenberg massacre, Matabele took three white children (never recovered) as curiosities to show Mzilikazi.

It was fortunate for the emigrant families that their leaders returned. Potgieter selected a hilltop as a defensive site, for he refused to be forced back. Some of the trekkers joined him in forming a laager, while others chose to retreat. When all the willing had come in, the effective count was forty men (guns) for the voortrekker stand at Vechtkop.

The Boer wagons were set closely into a square laager, wheels and wagon tongues tied together and all openings between and beneath choked with thickets of thornbrush. Inside the square, other wagons formed an inner shield for children and for women not used as musket loaders. The defenders had enough powder, and the lead balls were slashed in a crisscrossed pattern by the women, so that a spread of deadly pellets would spew out.

Mzilikazi, meanwhile, dispatched a force of about five thousand warriors to overrun the Boers' defense, and to collect their remaining herds. Scouts alerted the Dutchmen that the northwest veld was black with approaching Matabele, and at dawn on October 16, 1836, the leaders went out on commando to meet the tribesmen. Sarel Cilliers was there:

> *Thirty-three of us left the laager to go and meet the Kaffirs, and found them about an hour and a half's distance on*

horseback from our camp. When they saw us, they quickly assembled and sat down orderly, and we rode to within fifty yards of them. I had a Hottentot who spoke the language well. I told him to speak loudly and distinctly with them, and why they had come to murder us, and rob us of our goods.

When they heard this, they all jumped upon their feet, and cried "Mzilikazi!" and only that word. We sprang from our horses and shot as fast as we could on the enemy. There was great confusion until the third round of fire, when they divided into two parties, so as to surround and close us in. As we had to fight with such a great enemy we had continually to retire, and then fight again before we reached our camp. I fired sixteen shots before coming to the laager; few of the shots missed, and I killed two or three in one shot.

The Matabele host came up and surrounded the wagon fort at a respectable distance. Separating into three masses, many squatted on their haunches and became immobile. A harsh hissing of loathing and battle anticipation assaulted Boer ears, as the blacks disposed themselves to a waiting war of nerves. In intervals between hissing surges, they whetted their assegai blades against stones in an ominous clatter. A herd of the Boers' cattle were driven up and slaughtered before the laager. The Matabele feasted on the raw, hot meat torn from the carcasses.

Inside the laager, guns were cleaned; positions assigned; powder and ball stocks allotted. The families joined Cilliers in a prayer meeting. Afterward, there was still no action—just the infernal sibilance pulsing in the heated air of midday. To break the suspense, the defenders tied a rag to the tip of a whip, and on cue it was cracked above the wagon tops. With a savage shout, the warriors leaped up and charged at the laagered wagons, beating a tattoo on their cowhide shields.

The action was indeed hot and heavy as the Matabele surged and

The laager defense at Vechtkop: forty guns versus five thousand spears.

attempted to overwhelm the wagons. But the defenders blasted away, maintaining the killing edge. The cooperation within remained swift and deft. "Give!" was the marksman's command as he laid down a smoking musket, and his women or elder children always had a primed weapon to pass to him. It is recorded that a Mrs. Swanepoel paused in the process as she saw a black arm waggling over the wagon's canvas, seeking leverage to roll on over. She slashed with a hatchet and the severed hand tumbled inside, but the body stayed outside. The laager was not penetrated!

Neither the Matabele nor the Zulu ever learned how to overcome the wagon forts. Their weapon system required physical contact for the killing thrust of the stabbing assegai. Their backup thrown assegais failed to effectively pierce the four-layered canvas stretched over the wagons. In frustration, many assegais were arched high with the hope they would impale a body in their fall. The successes these warriors claimed against the whites occurred in the open, and even so, rarely against horsemen, because of the commando's mobility and the distant death delivered from its guns.

The Matabele at Vechtkop surged in ineffective waves for about an hour. In the ebbs between assaults, the Boers kept up their fire as they detected survivors in the drifts of bodies outside. Eventually, with an ascending hiss of frustration, the warriors broke off the siege and, driving the captured herds, started back to Mosega. A brave Boer patrol immediately followed, harrying, attempting to cut out cattle and oxen, but without success. Sarel Cilliers summed up:

The waggon in which I was had seventy-two stabs in the canvas. When the fight was over, two men had been killed on our side, and fourteen wounded, of whom I was one. * *Round the camp, 430 of the enemy lay dead. 1,175 assegais had been thrown into the camp. Two horses were killed, one wounded.*

The enemy then carried off all our means of sustenance. I had a wife and seven children, and was without corn or millet, besides being incapacitated for hunting. . . . My children cried from hunger, and I did the same, and had nothing to give them. *

The Boer relief party arrived from Thaba Nchu fifteen days after the Vechtkop battle, bringing oxen to withdraw the immobilized wagons. Falling back to Thaba Nchu, Potgieter's gaunt veterans were heartened to find a large new trek group under Gert Maritz had

*[Cilliers received an assegai in the knee, wrenched it out and killed his attacker.]

come up from the colony, and Piet Retief would soon follow.

Potgieter was desperate to regain his group's cattle, so much so that he asked the aid of the Cape Colony government. But that same year the pro-Bantu British Colonial Office had approved a friendship pact with Mzilikazi! So the Boers, in January 1837, dispatched their own 107-man commando on a daring five-hundred-mile circuit north to surprise the Matabele at their Mosega headquarters and recover over five thousand cattle. Indeed, in the next year Potgieter's commandos would defeat and drive the Matabele permanently beyond the Limpopo River boundary. The Transvaal lands were thereafter the white tribe's domain.

The voortrekkers spent much of 1837 attempting to form a viable nation. By May there were about one thousand trek wagons in the Orange River district. Recent events in the Cape Colony had all tended to reinforce the secessionists' wish to separate.

The next Xhosa border conflict followed the course of others. The early murderous, destructive Bantu raiding into the colony was blocked and then turned back by English troops and Boer commandos. The Xhosa warriors and people were driven far behind the Fish River boundary. This time the English governor dared to annex the territory with intent to open it to white settlement.

But the British government, still under the influence of the LMS, issued a stinging rejection of the governor's policy. The border war was the fault, not of the natives, but of greedy colonists, declared London. The conquered land must be returned to the Xhosa tribe, and the cost to the government of the conflict was to be recovered by the sale of the cattle retrieved as war spoils. Little wonder that Piet Retief, having published a popular list of the farmers' grievances, gathered a substantial following and arrived at the Thaba Nchu rendezvous in what was to become the Orange Free State as a candidate for supreme trek leader.

At fifty-six, Retief was the oldest of the prominent trek leaders, a man who through personality and actions had always been popular, though his business career had followed a boom-and-bust cycle. As

a planner, Retief tended to err on the side of optimism and gullibil-
ity. In his campaigning around Thaba Nchu, doing spade work to
turn the trek groups into a unified political as well as spiritual nation,
he found the ground hard. Having acquired a strong individuality in
their social isolation, the voortrekkers were further separated by the
jealousies of their leaders. They would not yet yield to real governmental authority. Proclamations of union and joint prayer meetings
were greeted with enthusiasm, but a tax system was unacceptable.
It took an emergency to unite the groups to action.

There was sharp disagreement as to where the nation, the Boers'
promised land, lay. Retief, Maritz, and Uys all were hot for Natal,
but the formidable pioneer Potgieter held out for the lands across
the Vaal River, the Transvaal. Natal lay beside the Indian Ocean,
he reminded Retief, and the English were always on the sea. As their
leaders wrangled, some of the trekkers settled there in the Orange
River area. Restless, some partisans voted with their feet as Potgieter
and his followers trekked back to the far-north Transvaal. Arriving,
they were disappointed that Louis Tregardt and his families were no
longer there.

The original trekker had become a belated casualty of Potgeiter's
stand-off with Matabeles. The isolated Boer colony had relied upon
Potgieter's promise to resupply them, but he had been delayed for
many months by the Matabele war. Their critical shortage was
gunpowder, and when they could wait no longer, Tregardt led his
group eastward down into Mozambique, seeking a trading connection for the ivory the Boers had stockpiled. Unaccustomed to the
unhealthy tropical coastlands, the travelers became infected with
fevers. Nearly all the men, including Louis Tregardt, died. The
Portuguese eventually returned the last survivors of the families to
the Cape Colony.

In the fall of 1837, Piet Retief announced he would make a
reconnaissance mission into Natal. Hundreds of emigrants were
ready to follow him at the slightest encouragement. First, a way had
to be searched out into Natal from the Boer interior. Around the

Boer trekkers cross the Drakensberg Mountains into Retief's promised land of Natal.

Orange River headwaters, the high veld broke off into a jagged mountain ridge, the Drakensberg (dragon mountains). Retief's scouts found passes through the cliffs where, with ingenuity, wagons could be roped down, or dragged up the thousand-foot inclines above the lush landscape of Natal.

Having established friendly contacts with the mountain Bantu, confident Piet Retief visited the small English enclave of Port Natal (modern Durban). Yes, he was told, the Boers would be welcomed as neighbors and users of their seaport. The merchants well understood this commercial opportunity. Retief pushed on to the Zulu chief, Dingane's, royal kraal, ignoring white warnings about black treachery. Retief said that he well knew how to deal with kaffirs.

Dingane, Shaka's slayer and successor, feared the coming of the Boers. He had heard about the Matabeles' disasters. But the Zulu king parleyed smoothly with Retief. Yes, he'd deed the whites a choice strip of land, said Dingane, but they'd have to do something for him first. A raiding party from the Batlokoa tribe in the mountains had run off a herd of Zulu cattle. Since these interlopers rode horses, wore parts of white man's clothing, and carried a few muskets, they must be allies of the Boers. Regain my cattle, proposed the king; prove your friendship, and I'll reward your service. Retief agreed.

As the Dutchmen departed, Dingane sent word to an upcountry *induna* to ambush and murder the whites. In practical African politics, Dingane saw it as: Kill before I am killed. But that Zulu commander feared the whites more than Dingane, for he disobeyed his monarch and fled with his followers toward sanctuary with the English at Port Natal. The lucky Retief proceeded unknowing, making plans. The Boers were on friendly terms with Chief Sikonyela of the Batlokoa tribe. Regaining the cattle would be easy.

It was: Having greeted the chief, Retief showed him a shiny metal plaything—handcuffs! They were snapped on the befuddled Bantu leader. Immobilized, he was lectured on the stolen cattle and detained until all, and then some, of the herd had been turned over to Zulus who had accompanied the Dutch. When they returned, these eyewitnesses told Dingane about the white magic that had paralyzed Chief Sikonyela. The result was that the Zulu king became frightened and more dangerous.

Word had already spread of Piet Retief's great expectations, and family wagons were skidding down the Drakensberg in numbers to await the signal to begin a land rush. Retief wanted to make a grand impression on Dingane when he went back to get the emigrants' land treaty signed, so he called for volunteers to make a procession, gathering sixty-six good men and true. Also, about thirty servants were enlisted.

Gert Maritz, the other prominent trek leader in Natal, disagreed with Retief's plan and voiced his suspicion of Zulu treachery. In a selfless gesture, he offered to go in Retief's place, accompanied by

a few men, so that if tragedy came, the Boers' loss would be mini-
mized. Retief would have none of it. His parting salutation to Maritz: "Farewell, you old coward!"

When Retief's ambassador commando appeared at Dingane's
royal kraal, they put on a military show of precision riding, punc-
tuated with deafening volleys of musketry. The Zulu king responded
with his own cast-of-thousands productions: dances, parades, and
feasting that went on for three days. In the negotiating sessions that
interspersed the merriment, Dingane sparred with the Dutchmen:
How was it that they had not killed Chief Sikonyela, or better,
brought him for Dingane to kill at his leisure? Retief's profession of
charity to Sikonyela was too foolish to be accepted. No! And now
that he, Dingane, had seen the white man's military show, how
about a gift of Sikonyela's horses and muskets?

Pointing to his gray hair, Retief retorted to the interpreter: "Tell
your master that I am not a child." Losing interest in the pretended
negotiations, the king became very agreeable. The whites could keep
for themselves the cattle they had recovered from the Batlokoa tribe,
said Dingane, and then he signed the land treaty in good humor. But
he insisted his new friends had to attend a ceremonial breakfast
before they departed in the morning.

At Dingane's kraal, there lived an English missionary family and
a white youth, who was an interpreter. Both specially warned the
Boers that Zulu gossip agreed the strangers would not leave alive.
But Retief and the others were on a roll of confident optimism.
Besides this, they had not, in their usually austere lives, enjoyed such
a good time as the Zulus were giving them.

Early on the morning of February 6, 1838, the entire Boer party
appeared for their last taste of Zulu hospitality. They left horses and
guns in the charge of their servants, went in to the royal presence,
and sat down to a breakfast topped off with fine Zulu beer. Dingane
had two disarmed *impis* on hand to entertain the guests by mass
dancing. The beguiled visitors did not react when the warriors concluded by wildly beating the battle tattoo on their shields. At the

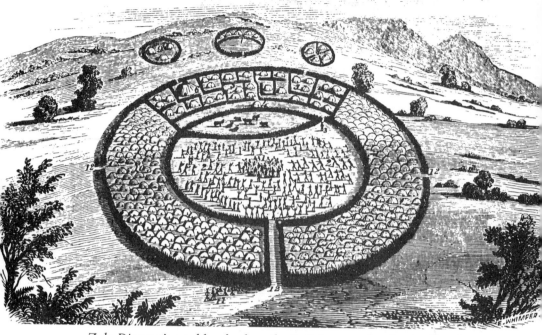

Zulu Dingane's royal kraal, where the Retief party enjoyed a fatal breakfast.

last, Dingane danced, his tall, corpulent figure swaying gracefully. When he, too, ceased, there was an expectant hush before Dingane gestured and sonorously shouted:

"Kill the wizards!"

Each guest was seized by three or four exdancers, was subdued and dragged out to the execution hill that since Shaka's days was a normal part of Zulu royal kraals. There, amid scores of rotting corpses, the killing proceeded. Retief was boosted up by his captors, the better to see the fate of his followers (including a son) before his own. The men were clubbed to death, afterward ripped and impaled with stakes. All of their servants were also killed, so the toll was about one hundred, and the hill was blackened by feeding vultures.

Dingane dispatched three *impis* northward as fast as they could trot. In the postmidnight blackness, they attacked the exposed, unguarded wagons of the eager Boer families awaiting Retief's good news. Only Maritz's camp was on alert further back and able to repulse the onslaught. Mass killing and savage mutilations went on for hours before the Zulus departed, driving off some ten thousand Boer cattle, and leaving behind some five hundred hacked and slashed bodies, including 185 children, 56 women, 40 men among the trekkers, and about two hundred of their servants. The name of the village later founded there memorialized the massacre. It was called Weenen (the weeping).

In the following dreary months, the Natal trekkers were immobilized in the rainy winter on short rations and stalked by sickness in the cramped communal laagers. Gert Maritz rallied and held them from mass retreat before he sickened and died. Help came from the northern voortrekker communities. Hendrik Potgieter came down to aid militarily. With Piet Uys, a commando unit was organized to strike south into Zululand to attempt to get back their vital resource of livestock.

Potgieter and Uys, having been on commando together before, knew they could only get along by ordering their own followers, though they rode together. Contact was made with a Zulu army, which retreated, luring the Dutchmen into rough, hilly countryside. The conservative Potgieter held back from the trap that it was, but Uys plunged into the thick of it. Soon encircled by native warriors, Uys's unit made an emergency breakout gallop that cost them ten men, including Uys. The Boer retreat became general and headlong, and this became known as the *vlugcommando*—the one that flew away. Potgieter was not a popular man in Natal and went back to his Transvaal in a huff.

Then, in November's South African springtime, a new Boer hero arrived in Natal. Andreis Pretorius came from the Cape Colony leading a new emigrant group. Fresh and vigorous, Pretorius publicly insisted there was an obvious solution they must get on with: Smash the Zulu power! Take their vast herds and flocks! Raising enthusiasm for gain and revenge, Pretorius organized a five-hundred-man commando and started south with sixty-four wagons.

The Zulu collected a huge army that lurked ahead of the Boer force, seeking an opportunity to attack. Pretorius helped them out. He chose a superb defensive position in an angle of the Ncome River and a tributary stream entering it through a gorge. Placing the sixty-four wagons in a crescent across the open side, the Dutch had room enough inside the laager to stable all horses and oxen. Transvaal veteran Sarel Cilliers was also there, and at a fervent religious service he exhorted the commando to swear to build a church there if God granted them life and success of arms.

When the morning mist lifted from the river bottomland on December 16, 1838, the five hundred with guns looked out upon ten thousand to fifteen thousand warriors with spears. The fight proceeded like the battle at Vechtkop, with tremendous slaughter of the Zulu in vain charges against the barricaded wagons. Then, when the Zulu paused in exhausted frustration, Pretorius charged out with nearly all of his force, broke the Zulu battle order, and pursued their fleeing army. The battle, or execution, lasted three hours, as the Dutch slew three thousand of Dingane's finest warriors. The river turned crimson in response. Ever afterward this turning-point engagement would be called Blood River.

Boer casualties were solely four wounded, including the aggressive Pretorius. Dingane abandoned his capital, leaving it in flames. The commando returned north with substantial herds and assurance that Natal was their promised land. The Zulu power system was destroyed by this defeat. Soon, Mpande, brother of Dingane, came over to the Boers with seventeen thousand Zulu followers. After more battles and retreats, Dingane ended as a fugitive, tortured to death by a minor Bantu chief.

Pretorius and the Natal trekkers proclaimed a republic at their new capital of Pietermaritzburg. The emigrants in the now-settled and peaceful Transvaal and Orange River lands also functioned independently. But as the Boers celebrated the apparent success of their secession, the Great Trek, they had to wonder what England might do to spoil it.

6

Disasters and Windfalls

Was the Great Trek a national disaster? Not according to the Boers, who believed it to be a successful vindication of past injustice and a threshold opportunity for a God-chosen people. The British government, however, was ambivalent and pondered for years the political consequences. But the Boers' secession ripped an enduring tear into the national fabric. It dispersed, and divided by cultural creed, peoples who needed uniting; it seeded war where there could have been continued peace; and it postponed for seventy years a common South African government. The stability the white settlement brought to the high veld prompted renewal among the Zulu-battered Bantu tribes.

The initial English reaction was confined to a warning that the trekkers remain British subjects and accountable to that government for their actions. Dr. Philip's London Missionary Society was distressed: Inspectors were sent out to learn whether the trekboers enslaved native tribes and violated the civil rights of the servants they brought out of the Cape Colony. They interviewed the servants, and found few had gone unwillingly.

In the Boer hinterlands, laborers were gathered by negotiation with local black chieftans, which was little different than the process of "catching" slaves. A common ploy, which outraged the

79

humanitarians in London, was recruitment of Bantu and Bushmen children, "orphans" of battles or tribal dispersions. These children remained for ten to fifteen years in farmer apprenticeships, until they were of age. In remote areas, these young people were marketable between farmers during the period of their apprenticeship. But there seems to be little evidence that they were mistreated.

Though the immigrant Dutch tolerated American and European missionaries in their new lands, there was little Christian love for, or from, the English churchmen, who were often expelled from Boer territory. Dr. David Livingstone, the future explorer, was a medical missionary resident just west of the Transvaal border in about 1850, an advisor to a Bantu chieftan whose quarrels with his Boer neighbors were continuous. Dr. Livingstone was equally partisan: "Resistance to such tyrants and murderers is, I think, obedience to God." He also wrote: "Malaria is not an unmitigated evil, since it swept off many Boers."

Most missionaries supplemented their income with business sidelines. Dr. Livingstone was a spare-time gunsmith, and the Boers raged that he was a gunrunner to Bantu savages! Dr. Livingstone wrote that he boasted about arming his natives with five hundred rifles and a cannon, lies told to deter the Dutch from attacking his friends. He actually supplied the Bantu with only a few hunting rifles, he said. But during native troubles, and while their missionary champion was absent on a trip, a Boer raid on Dr. Livingstone's workshop turned up, they said, a stockpile of about fifty guns.

It was a report of child slavery that publicly urged the British toward the annexation of Natal. Andreis Pretorius's last Zulu-smashing expedition, called the *beestecommando* because the Dutchmen captured eighty thousand cattle, also returned with about a thousand Zulu orphans. This acquisition of new servants drew bad publicity in London and Capetown. Then, when the Boers found cause to attack a tribe living in the Xhosa region (toward the Cape Colony's troubled eastern border), Britain moved into Natal to guarantee native rights in their relations with the Boers.

Missionary David Livingstone: gunrunner to the natives?

But the annexation's most important reasons were political and economic. Coal had been discovered in Natal, and this was the beginning of the steamship age. If there was coaling of foreign shipping to be done, it should be under the British colors and for English profit. American vessels (mostly whalers) had been calling at Durban; Britain regarded Yankee foreign maneuvering with jealous suspicion in the nineteenth century. Also, taking Natal would bottle up the Boers inland, making them subject to British trade tariffs.

So a small British army moved into Natal. A commando under Pretorius came down to the coast, and there was a skirmish that the smaller invading force lost. If Pretorius had had the fortitude to push the soldiers of great Great Britain into the Indian Ocean, he might then have had done with it. However, the Boer commander contented himself with a siege. Just as it appeared that the English were starved to the point of surrender, their reinforcing troop ships arrived in Port Natal's bay. Pretorius retreated cautiously, and soon (1843) the Boer Republic in Natal was extinguished. Many families turned about and trekked back over the Drakensberg into the two other Boer territories of Orange River and Transvaal. Old Hendrik Potgieter had been right: "On the sea are always the English."

In the Cape Colony, another Kaffir War broke out at the end of 1846 on the eastern frontier. The latest surge of the crowded Xhosa nation was at length subdued in 1847 and peace was restored, but with a difference: The long-standing colonial policy of not enclosing Bantu tribal lands was overturned. The man who did it was Sir Harry Smith, the new, militant governor of the Cape Colony. Sir Harry was a career soldier who had directed the colony's defense in an earlier Kaffir War, then had gone out to India and to great triumphs that earned him knighthood.

Governor Smith assembled the defeated Xhosa chieftans and showed them a wagon standing alone. At his signal the munition-stuffed vehicle exploded spectacularly, terrifying the native audience, illustrating what would happen to them if they renewed the war. Then he gripped a wad of reribboned parchment, tore it apart, and scattered the fragments downwind. So much for past treaties! From now on the tribes were settled in restricted enclaves under the eyes of colonial overseers. A surge of English and European emigrants occupied the windfall of emptied Xhosa lands.

The age of native reservations had come to South Africa, even as it had in the United States. The situation in America of fewer Indians and many whites was reversed in proportion and volume in Africa, where the black majority was inside the reserves, the white minority outside. The Xhosa tribes would, when recovered, test Sir Harry's wagon and help run him out of the country; but over in Natal the whites were aided by the long life of the friendly Zulu chief Mpande, and the emergence there of Theophilus Shepstone as a talented white *induna* who would personally maintain peace with the Zulus for thirty-six years.

In 1848, Governor Smith began to pay attention to the Boer republics. The Orange River republic's government was weak and, in the trekker fashion, full of contention. Smith did not have to seek for evidence of turmoil. There was recurring black/white strife over exceptionally fertile land just below the mountain stronghold of the neighboring, now powerful, Basuto nation. Both Bantu and Boer would benefit from orderly Colonial Office supervision, Sir Harry reasoned, so he extended Britannia's rule by creating a new colony: The Orange River Sovereignty.

The emigrant Boers were riled and rallied into a commando led by Andreis Pretorius, which occupied the principal town of Bloemfontein. Sir Harry was not too perturbed at this local hostility for two reasons: He recalled that Pretorius had backed out before the British in Natal; and Smith believed correctly that the other Boer state, Transvaal, would stand aside, hoping thereby that Britain, in return, would allow its independent survival.

General Smith himself came up with English troops and met and defeated Pretorius in a sharp skirmish at Boomplaats. Pretorius's Boers didn't want a real war with the British. The resistance collapsed and, as a fugitive with Sir Harry's ten-thousand-dollar bounty out for him, Pretorius fled into Transvaal. England ruled (1848) at Orange River, and in 1852 rewarded Transvaal's neutrality by officially recognizing its existence.

The Colonial Office in London approved Smith's annexations as an economy move. The politicians in power there were not happy about a poor, money-draining colony like South Africa. It was too late to get rid of it altogether, but at least he could cut expenses!

One primary expense was the keeping of troops there to protect the Cape Colony and the high cost of fighting its recurring native wars. Sir Harry staked his official future on keeping a Bantu-Boer-Briton peace by placing the natives on supervised reserves and firmly ruling the Boers, who otherwise might blunder into a great Bantu war, which must then, expensively, draw in the British.

But the Xhosa nation had already spoiled Smith's plan by 1850. Crammed into reserves, which were also stuffed with other native refugees since Shaka's time and also accommodated a resettlement of Hottentots, the tensions needed only a provocation like drought to begin a revolt. The home government's policy of economy meant there were meager troops available for Sir Harry's counterattack. The Eighth Kaffir War dragged on, and Governor Smith lost his credibility in London. He was recalled (1852) and replaced by another governor of military background, Sir George Cathcart.

Meanwhile the Basuto tribes in the Orange River Sovereignty continued warlike. A government commando sent to subdue them was defeated. Reinforcement was needed, to the chagrin of the British Colonial Office. Orange River seemed to the Colonial Office to have no worth. It was a rather arid, high plain inhabited by country bumpkins who refused to speak the queen's English.

In 1854, Great Britain actually backed out of this colony. The Boer republic was reborn as the Orange Free State, basing its constitution on the American model, and it made some civic progress during the long presidency of Johannes H. Brand.

The new Cape governor, General Cathcart, briskly finished Sir Harry's task of subduing, for the eighth time, the blacks, then was recalled to England to serve in the Russian war (1854), where he died. In the middle fifties, the settlers around the Xhosa reserves fearfully awaited a ninth Kaffir War.

The frustrated natives, unable to defeat the whites, sought victory via supernatural intervention. Young women had visions, and the witch doctor Mhlakaza interpreted their hysteria. The long-dead chiefs and heroes of the Xhosa lore had risen from the dead and were vengeful, according to Mhlakaza. They were called "Russians" and had killed their late oppressor, Cathcart, in the land beyond the sea. Now they were coming to the homeland and would drive out the whites forever. *But* they required, in advance, great evidence of their peoples' pledge of belief in their supernatural powers. As in many religions, this was to be accomplished by the rite of sacrifice in acknowledgement and exchange for the greater God-given good.

The witch doctor announced that all cattle were to be slaughtered, no crops were to be planted, and any food stores remaining must be destroyed before August 16, 1856. If the nation purified itself by that date, the great chiefs would return, bringing with them bigger, better cattle, corn, guns, and wagons. Two suns would rise and a mighty whirlwind would sweep the white race into the depths of the sea, Mhlakaza prophesied.

Because of the presence of agents in the reservations, the Cape government knew of the phenomenon early on and strove to defeat the superstition. Agent Charles Brownlee rode tirelessly among the tribes, emphasizing so vehemently that the prophesies would *never* occur, that the natives nicknamed him Napakade (never!). He achieved partial success; the cattle killing went ahead by tribes. Some killed zealously, others held off. In August, English troops were moved into visible positions to show that they had not been wiped out by the Russians, and to keep order should there be turmoil on the Great Day.

August 16 was a witch doctor's dud. The chiefs had not come, Mhlakaza declared, because the Xhosa had not thoroughly shown their worthiness. After consulting two young seeresses, he set December 31 as the new apocalypse. Hunger was appearing among the people, and some unbelievers guiltily killed their cattle. Still, the new year came in uneventfully, and, finally, on February 10, 1857, Mhlakaza raged that the ancestors were very angry because their children were holding back on them. They had eight days—or never!

Desperately, the very hungry Xhosa believers "stabbed their cattle to the very last one and left their carcases as food for vultures and wild dogs." They dug new corn pits to receive the promised bounty and tied down thatched roofs so they would not blow away in the whirlwind. But February 18, 1857, was another blue-sky summer day; no miracles disturbed the sun's passage from horizon to horizon. The witch doctor said that the chiefs had quarreled among themselves and therefore had not come. And he shut up.

Near and real, starvation enveloped the Xhosa reserves. The government offered relief, but it was far from sufficient for the very many. Mrs. Brownlee wrote of the "breathing skeletons" who thronged their government station:

Daily, as these spectres came in crowds and crawled along, one might have imagined that the prophet's prediction had come to pass, and that the dead had indeed risen from their graves.

During 1857, the population in the district of British Kaffraria plummeted from 104,000 to 37,000. Of the missing, a third at least were reckoned dead. However, out of the Xhosa disaster, the colonists gained two windfalls: the end of cohesive Xhosa tribal threats; and the immigration into the Cape Colony of about thirty thousand very willing laborers.

In the 1860s it was discovered that the hot, humid seaside lowlands 'of Natal could be profitably set to sugar cane. However, cane cutting was a more physical task than cattle herding, and the resident Zulu would not do this work. Slavery was unlawful, but the English proprietors found a near-slave solution by importing laborers from India. The oppressive caste system there made those at the social-economic bottom desperately willing to cross oceans and do plantation labor cheaply on long contracts in British Empire colonies like Trinidad, Fiji, and Natal. About sixty-four hundred were imported, men and women, few of whom ever returned to India. Thus a new nationality had been added to the national unmelting pot.

At the end of 1860s, a sparkling windfall dazzled South Africa, and soon the world.

On a spring day in 1866, beside the Orange River, about 450 miles north of Capetown, fifteen-year-old Erasmus Jacobs rested under a tree after a farm chore. Idly, the lad picked up a small, strangely glittering white stone. He carried it home and gave the curio to a younger sister. Mother Jacobs noticed its sparkle and showed the object to a neighbor, Schalk van Niekerk, who had a few connections with the outside world.

Van Niekerk offered a token payment but his embarrassed hostess pressed the curio freely into his hand; it was just a stone, after all. A farm-to-farm peddler, Jack O'Reilly, agreed to find out if it had value. Eventually the stone arrived (by post in an unsealed letter) at the office of the nearest competent geologist, W. G. Atherstone, who certified it as a *diamond* with a value (approximately, in dollar conversion) of twenty-five hundred dollars. Governor Wodehouse of the Cape Colony purchased the "Eureka" diamond at that price; it was sent to the Paris Exposition of 1867.

A slight diamond rush of neighboring Orange Free State Boers had disappointing results. The prospectors had not seen what they were looking for! Interest waned, for prominent geologists pooh-poohed the notion of diamonds in South Africa. It was a misunderstanding or a fluke, they asserted. Absolutely.

Rare as a diamond in South Africa was the likelihood that Mr. van Niekerk should have a second chance at a diamond fortune, but so it turned out. An adult Hottentot shepherd, Swartbooi, found (1869) a large diamond in the rough. He showed the unusual white stone to his witch doctor, happily an honest practitioner, who sent him on to see van Niekerk, the only man still interested in glittering white stones. The Hottentot, who considered himself as not born yesterday, boldly started the bargaining at an impossible figure: two thousand dollars cash up front.

Van Niekerk, like any farmer, held little cash, so he offered Swartbooi his livestock resource—five hundred sheep, ten oxen, and a horse. A horse alone could represent a Hottentot's life savings. So

Swartbooi accepted. Van Niekerk sold the diamond stone to a merchant of Hopetown for about fifty thousand dollars. The forty-seven-carat "Star of South Africa" became an adornment of the Countess of Dudley for about one hundred fifty thousand dollars.

The rush was on! The local Boers had the advantage because they were closest. Many English came, as did seasoned prospectors from every mineral frontier in the world. India had been the traditional diamond source, then Brazil. Diamonds are found in alluvial places, riverbeds, and flood plains, so the shores of the Orange and Vaal rivers received the early brunt of searching and sluicing. Diamonds *were* found here and there, and soon the true diamond lode was prospected some miles away.

Diamonds are formed in the material filling ancient volcanic tubes, yellow and crumbly at the surface, turning blue and harder at about sixty feet down, and descending an unknown distance into the earth's core. A cluster of four tubes, each just five hundred to a thousand feet in surface diameter, became the early focus of the miners, and they were bonanzas. The three farms enclosing them were soon sold off for about fifty thousand dollars (in twenty years their value was fifty million dollars). The De Beers brothers, who received about thirty-three thousand dollars, had paid one hundred fifty dollars for their farm.

A communal Diggers' Committee governed the diamond sites efficiently. It was agreed that claim work areas would be thirty-foot squares. Disputes were adjusted principally by fisticuffs. Seldom was there violence with gun or knife. The mining method was to dig down within the square, winching out buckets of earth to be sieved and searched for diamonds.

A young Englishman named Cecil Rhodes mined a claim with his elder brother. As the pits deepened (the "big hole" at Kimberley is four hundred feet deep), water seepage bothered the diggers. It was young Rhodes's inspiration to import a steam pump, and, on a service fee basis, he managed his start toward fortune and fame.

The town that sprang up in tents among the diamond pipes was called Kimberley, for the then-English colonial secretary. The Orange Free State had the legitimate claim, but the English backed an older territory named Griqualand West, with a poorly marked boundary, and put in its claim. Meanwhile, Transvaal made a half-serious attempt to take over the diamond area by presidential decree, sending down a high-level official commando. Unwelcomed, they chose to withdraw after receiving a threat of being lynched! Briefly, a Diggers' Republic was proclaimed, with an ex-sailor, Stafford Parker, as president.

The English moved in, using the time-honored plea of "protection of the natives." Lord Keate, the Natal governor, judged the rival Griqualand and Orange Free State claims. The Griqua won, of course, and Griqualand West-expanded was immediately absorbed into the Cape Colony (1871). The British could scarcely believe it—South Africa had become a paying proposition.

The Orange Free State had been robbed. However, the overview is that its simple pastoral government could not have coped with the complications of international finance beginning in Kimberley. The Orange president Brand nagged the English for years, until a settlement of half a million dollars was paid. Also, for nearly thirty years the little Boer state would prosper by providing supplies to the nearby diamond industry.

Diggers' Committee, Diggers' Republic—yes, but those gentlemen scarcely soiled their hands. The spade diggers were black, brown, yellowish—any hue but white. The traditional division was imposed as quickly as possible in the diamond mines: The blacks labored cheaply while the whites supervised and profited. Observer W. J. Martin noted:

Dress suit and society paraphernalia are indispensible. . . . An abundant supply of negro labour allows men of education and capital to engage in the occupation of "digging." This word must therefore be dissociated from the conventional idea of roughness and lawlessness.

As this start to the industrial revolution took place in South Africa, the blacks were installed at the bottom. Since Boers were in charge at the outset, no native was allowed to possess a diamond, nor own or operate a claim. Under English colonial administration, the color bar was lifted officially. However, in practice, few native entrepreneurs appeared. They needed a certificate of good and responsible character issued by a local magistrate (likely a Boer), and even if they passed this considerable hurdle, they lacked the capital investment. Fifteen years after the discoveries, native operators amounted to about ten percent of the small, independent diggers.

The men on the shovels earned as much as eight dollars a month plus room and board (1871). Being unused to money, they tended to spend it quickly on adornments and Cape Smoke, the powerful, cheap raw liquor. Intoxication led to absenteeism, and then to a law that the native must have his master's permission to obtain spirits—not an effective measure. A bit later, the supply of labor was stabilized by an ingenious mine operator's offer: Work at least three months, and obtain a gun and ammunition. The "bush telegraph" worked efficiently, and the labor supply was assured.

Out in the native reserves or farther afield in the wilderness, the realization had come to the chiefs that there was no respectability anymore without the white man's firearms. Collecting a supply, formerly a catch-as-catch-can affair, was now an open opportunity at the Kimberley mines (by one claim, 300,000 were distributed).

So the mine labor supply was actively and persistently recruited by the chiefs and sent trudging their hot, dusty way to the mines, likely hundreds, even a thousand miles away, to work their contract and march back proudly bearing a rifle and cartridge band. The journey was exhausting, sometimes fatal. Little aid could be expected from the Boers along the way. Eyewitness Martin describes a Kimberley street scene:

A stream of foot passengers lines the sidewalks, while along the centre of the streets crowds of naked negroes, often singing their weird songs, go to and fro from their work.

*Or perhaps, a gang of "raw" natives, just down thousands of
miles from the countries of the North, dusty, thin as skeletons, foot-sore, dirty and strange with barbaric utensil and
ornament, thread their way along, hooted at, and pelted with
dirt and stones by their initiated countrymen. This reception
of the neophyte is of daily occurrence, and the ear can readily
follow the direction pursued by the entering band by listening
for the succession of derisive yells which greet it at each step
of its progress.*

Two problems of native labor presented themselves in the early
1870s: It was estimated that the workers stole half of the diamonds
they discovered! The stones were frequently small and easily con-
cealed in body orifices. Many were swallowed. Those suspected of
this were forcibly fed emetics and laxatives to retrieve the wealth.
But daily passing in and out of digging sites made it easy to deliver
many stones into the substantial network of native and, eventually,
white receivers. But digging or stealing, the laborer got no more than
a pittance.

The other problem was widespread drunkeness, which, besides
reducing manpower, raised some possibility of mass rioting.

The solution was the compound, easing both complaints. A
fenced, patrolled barracks area near the work site became the restricted home turf where the native spent his time when not on the
job. Alcoholic usage was successfully monitored there, and the
search for contraband diamonds and/or the opportunity to transport
them was reduced to a single time at the end of the worker's contract. It is reported that the compound inhabitants came around to
favor the arrangement. It conserved worker income, as well as their
physical condition, for it was noted that the natives departed the
mines as better, healthier specimens than when they arrived.

The advancing 1870s saw much overseas investment and consoli-
dation of the diamond industry. Digging was replaced by deep shafts
and tunneling at the corporate sites. The individual digger claim had
vanished from the lucrative "dry diggings" of Kimberley. Corporate

Caught swallowing a diamond!

builders and raiders warred on paper battlefields for control of the mines, and thereby manipulation of the diamond market. The centuries-old pace of the ox was challenged in the heartland by the rising whirr of the rock drill. These pressures shaped two striking opposing leaders, and it is time now to consider them both: Paul Kruger and Cecil Rhodes.

7

The Fated Adversaries

Cecil Rhodes and Paul Kruger walked onto the South African national stage in the 1870s. During the following twenty years, they became the area's dominant opposing personalities in the escalating conflict between Briton and Boer: the former for mastery, the latter for survival. In background, personality, and philosophy, Kruger and Rhodes aptly characterized the clashing white cultures in South Africa—Kruger's static rural conservatism versus Rhodes's dynamic industrial imperialism.

The elder of the adversaries was Paul Kruger, born into a Cape Colony frontier farmer's family on October 10, 1825. Paul's formal education was modest—just three months of instruction by an itinerant teacher. His father tutored Paul in reading the Bible, wherein he learned to fear and love God unconditionally. Young Paul grew up ignorant of or antagonistic toward the social and scientific ideas that had flourished in the European Enlightenment since 1700. To Kruger, the earth was flat, with God daily directing the sun's journey across it. If it were otherwise, the Bible would have told him so.

To the pious Boer in his preferred self-reliant isolation upon the wild veld, all social problems were readily solved by reference to the Bible, and within the strict patriarchal family order it endorsed. And to control the harsh realities of the outside environment, its necessary or hostile animals and humans, the Boer had his guns. Bible and rifle: With just these, all of South Africa could be his. Young Paul grew up devout and could shoot creditably at age seven. When he was fourteen he killed his first lion.

In politics, the Kruger family shared the frontier aversion to the English strangers, which was reinforced by later laws and actions. When Hendrik Potgieter proposed to trek northward, the Krugers went along. It is not known whether, at twelve, Paul was a gun-loader in the desperate laager at Vechtkop, but as a youthful warrior he did ride north with the Potgieter commando that raided the Matabele stronghold at Mosega and retrieved their cattle. Thus, Kruger was able to declare that when he was fourteen he had slain both his first lion and his first kaffir.

Paul Kruger is revered as the George Washington of the Afrikaners and many stories are told about his youthful triumphs, feats of strength, endurance, and toughness.

Once in close quarters with an African water buffalo, which after the elephant and rhinoceros is the most muscularly powerful of animals, Paul's gun misfired. He sprang away as the buffalo charged, but sank, momentarily mired in a mud hole. The creature was instantly upon him, butting. A horn tip missed and stuck into the mud. With both hands Kruger gripped the other horn and forced the buffalo's nostrils and mouth below the waterline. He had half-drowned the brute before it twisted free and ran from its dangerous opponent.

Once again, while shooting at a charging rhinoceros, the barrel of Kruger's rifle exploded, mangling his left hand. He ran ahead of the ponderous beast to where he had left his horse, and managed to remount, then with handkerchief clenched over the bleeding flesh, rode miles to the family wagon. He endured the excruciating burn of a dousing with turpentine to staunch the bleeding, then trimmed away the useless bone and flesh himself. Gangrene developed, and his life was in danger. As a last resort, a native cure was tried. A goat was slaughtered, its abdomen ripped open. Kruger plunged his fes-

The Rock of Ages: President Paul Kruger during the Boer War.

tering fist into the hot entrails, held it there, claiming to feel the discomfort draw out, and repeated the procedure with a second goat. The near-fatal infection waned and his hand healed.

Paul married at seventeen and suffered the loss of his wife and newborn child when he was twenty. His faith in God's unfailing goodness and subjection to His will were wrenched on this occasion, but after a week or so of wandering in the mountains, he emerged with a stronger faith than before.

Kruger remarried happily and fathered sixteen children; they rewarded his lineage with 120 grandchildren. In middle life he remained an exceptionally strong, bulky six-footer, a successful farmer, local patriarch, and sought-after commando leader when the Bantu needed punishing. He rose in Transvaal politics, and after Britain made its short-lived annexation of Transvaal, he traveled to London to vainly negotiate restoration of the Boer Republic.

Afterward, he was active in its successful revolt, and became Transvaal's president in 1883. Kruger fended off imperialists after the remarkable gold discoveries in Transvaal's Rand district in 1886 and later declared the Boer's war upon the British. Of Cecil Rhodes, he once remarked that little truth could be expected in negotiations with a nonfamily man who didn't attend church.

Cecil Rhodes was born a younger son into a rural English parson's large family on July 5, 1853 (Paul Kruger was already twenty-eight). His health was delicate, and as he showed a tendency to tuberculosis, he emigrated at eighteen to join an elder brother in Natal, South Africa. Before sailing, the youth borrowed the equivalent of ten thousand dollars from an indulgent aunt. Rhodes's arrival in South Africa coincided with the diamond rush, which the brothers soon joined. Cecil's capital investment fared well, for their diamond claims at Kimberley returned an average of five hundred dollars a week, according to a letter Cecil sent to England at this time.

Rhodes now pondered his future, what to make of it and how. He was excessively ambitious, and capital topped his requirements: "It is no use having big ideas if you have not the cash to carry them through." The money that he desired in great quantities was not for itself but as the means toward power. Capitalists were becoming preeminent in Europe and America. Men who controlled money ruled the world, for politicians and nearly everyone could be bought. The rise and decline of Rhodes's career is a study in the use of that axiom.

This precocious young man would be foremost among the upcoming breed of imperialists, the money movers and shakers who would see to the partition of the undeveloped world into national spheres to be exploited for the profit and glory of Western nations. Cecil Rhodes was a passionate imperialist Englishman: "I contend, that we are the first race in the world, and the more of the world we inhabit, the better it is for the human race."

Rhodes loved Africa as a theater for imperialist action; he envisioned it all the way from "Cape to Cairo." He sensed great undiscovered mineral wealth. Find it, control it, and set the "niggers" to digging it out. His views coincided here with the Boers': Take their land, and then their labor. Rhodes admired certain qualities in Kruger and his followers, though it developed that they alone were the persons who could not be "bought," because they rejected or could not understand any incentive he offered.

Rhodes decided early on that he should receive a college education, the very best; to him that meant Oxford. The ambitious young man had noted that Oxford graduates often reached "the top of the tree," and he wanted to be up there, too. So, for a few years, he divided his time between Kimberley and Oxford. He was able to enter one of Oxford's lesser colleges and attended satisfactorily. It has been said that at Oxford his mind was preoccupied with South African schemes, and when in Kimberley he yearned for Oxford's genteel atmosphere.

It was while in Oxford that Cecil developed his steam pump idea to make an early fortune servicing the waterlogged claims of diamond diggers. Then, at Oxford, Rhodes suffered a major heart attack and was warned that he probably would not live long. He returned to South Africa with a sense of urgency. There was much he must do. "The great fault of life," Rhodes declared with fervor, "is its shortness." Nor was there religious consolation. The preacher's son coolly considered the existence of God to be a fifty-fifty proposition. But Rhodes the tycoon expected to be remembered for four thousand years.

Rhodes is recalled as a bulky, blond six-footer, thick and square in outline, with ham hands, a double chin, sensual mouth, and heavy-lidded gray-blue eyes. In sum he appeared to be an old young man. Socially, he was a good mixer, a charmer through enthusiasm, gregarious with men (but *no* women). Rhodes cherished male friendships, and though he moved forward by buying men (amusedly naming horses in his stable after them), he didn't fear that his friends would sell him out.

Dr. Starr Jameson (left) *and his friend Cecil Rhodes during happy days in Kimberley.*

Ideas, and dreams that became schemes consumed his waking hours. He took no interest in bookkeeping detail, owned no safe, carried no pocket money, was perpetually overdrawn (although no bank refused him). Thinking big and acting accordingly; that was his life's meaning. His Kimberley lodgings were modest and unkempt; he was an untidy dresser, frequently seen in old white flannels. Impulsive, he laughed much, but had little understanding of humor; was quick to anger and to make amends. Many testified that Cecil Rhodes was true to his personal friends and didn't discard them as he moved up in fortune.

When Rhodes was twenty-seven (1880), he founded the De Beers Company, eventually *the* consolidator of the diamond industry. Initial capital investment was about one million dollars. Five years later the company was worth four million and paid a dividend of seven-and-a-half percent. Then in two years De Beers exploded to a worth of twelve million dollars, paying twenty-five percent.

That was after Rhodes linked up with Barney Barnato, another major force in the diamond industry. They had sparred for years, until Rhodes discovered their means of compromise: Barney wanted money, while Cecil wanted power. Barnato, risen from the slums of London, also craved status. Rhodes had become the premier club-man, and the buying of Barnato included the promotion by Rhodes of the colorful, lowborn capitalist to membership in Kimberley's exclusive club.

Rhodes's commercial actions were now matched by imperialist thinking in the Colonial Office, London. The "Little Englanders" had been turned out of office and replaced by Prime Minister Disraeli's empire expansionists. Now that South Africa had become profitable (in the nick of time, for the Suez Canal had cut the need to sail around Africa, and reduced Capetown's strategic importance), the Colonial Office wanted to maximize British influence: to bind all South Africa into a federation. London decided that two obstacles remained to be removed to smooth that transition.

First, Zululand. The paramount chief, Cetewayo, had increased

Barney Barnato, the flamboyant Randlord, in a caricature from Vanity Fair.

the Zulu warrior *impis* again to alarming size and efficiency and was acting at home like a real sovereign. By 1877, Cetewayo was quarreling with the Boers along their Transvaal border. He had not threatened Natal, but it was the English living there who felt most threatened. London calmly decided to cancel this threat by a preemptive military strike. A top general, Lord Chelmsford, was instructed to prepare and carry out the Zulu War.

The second obstacle: In the British plan, federation had to include the independent Boer republics. It was believed that the Orange Free State would come in; but Transvaal, far larger, was vaguely in opposition. Indeed, it was difficult to understand what went on in Transvaal. The Afrikaners there truly practiced the theory of "who governs least, governs best." As a result, there was a confused national policy, with no money in its treasury. The postmaster paid his own salary in stamps! Transvaal's currency had no practical value beyond its borders; and its latest expedition against the natives had been unsuccessful. London reasoned that this "nation" needed a British takeover, and maybe the English could walk right in.

Theophilus Shepstone of Natal, the wily overseer of the Zulu, was instructed to do it. He may have warned Cetewayo about the possibility of Boer agression; and then in Transvaal's capital of Pretoria convinced his hosts not to worry about a Zulu invasion, for England, in taking over, would see to that. He went to Pretoria with an imperial guard of twenty-five police and talked around; then he suddenly announced that a majority of the citizens favored a British takeover, and proclaimed it (1877). That he was able to do this showed how disorganized Transvaal's "government" really was. In its treasury, English auditors found twelve shillings, six pence.

But the surface appearance deceived. Although they were slow to react, Transvaalers certainly did not desire English rule. Their fathers had trekked north to escape it. Paul Kruger, emerging as the conservative nationalist leader, took as reliable a poll as could be managed in the country's wide-open spaces and concluded that about eighty percent of the settlers opposed Britain's action. Kruger journeyed to London with his report to attempt negotiation to restore Transvaal independence. It was a useless trip, and after Shepstone's departure, Colonel Owen Lanyon, a British army officer, ruled in Pretoria as if the land were his garrison. Afrikaner language and custom were ignored, and there was even an attempt to collect taxes! Gradually the British oppression brought together the disparate Afrikaner factions.

Meanwhile, top British officials in South Africa, provoked the Zulu War (1879), by ordering Chief Cetewayo to stop harassing (killing) certain of his Zulu subjects. The monarch replied that royal killing was correctly within the Zulu way of life, as it had been with their forefathers. He declared that he respected the English governor of Natal; let him respect King Cetewayo. Each was sovereign in territory and actions. A curt English ultimatum went unanswered. Lord Chelmsford's English army, in three spearheads, then invaded Zululand.

On the eve of the invasion, high British officials asked Paul Kruger, as a noted commando leader, for pointers on fighting the Zulus. He spoke wisely of the necessity of turning the wagons to laager at encampments and keeping savvy scouts out at a distance. Zulu *impis* were notably stealthy and swift, he warned. Kruger also made a political offer. He would recruit and lead a five-hundred-man Boer commando "and hand Zululand over to you, if you give me the reward I want." But that reward was Transvaal's independence; so he was refused and went home.

The English were excessively confident. They had guns—repeating rifles and cannons; the Zulu still relied on overwhelming manpower with spears, while belatedly collecting rifles. Lord Chelmsford felt he didn't need a rabble of frontier sharpshooters and he sensed no possibility of disaster as his central column moved unopposed a short day's march into the populous land of the Zulus.

This Empire force (about 4,700 troops) camped on a strip of plain or plateau below a rocky hill the Zulu called "Isandhlwana" because it resembled a distended cow's stomach. There was a good overlook toward the east where the Zulu army presumably lurked. No attention was paid to defenses within or without beyond normal sentries and unit preparedness. The night was uneventful, and in the morning the general and his best offensive troops set out on a deep reconnaissance to locate and engage the enemy. They passed some miles away from their base, drawn by flitting, retreating warriors, a Zulu bait.

Colonel Pulleine, with his remaining third of the force, thought of Isandhlwana as a rear support camp. He assumed the fighting would occur out front, where Lord Chelmsford roamed. It was too much work, unnecessary, to place the wagons in defensive laager. Scouts were not efficiently outposted either, and the ammunition cases were stacked below foodstuffs. Pulleine's detachment was idly waiting out the day looking forward to their comrades' triumphant return.

So the British camp was in an inviting, noncombatant position when at noon several Zulu *impis,* upward of ten thousand men, suddenly appeared at the sides and rear. The initial English fire killed many Zulus, but the defenders had no opportunity to reload or regroup. Historian C. E. Vulliamey declares: "Isandhlwana was not a battle, it was a butchery." The massacre killed about 1,300 Empire troops, of whom some 850 were British. No one who stood and fought survived. And this battle day was not over; next was Rorke's Drift (ford).

For Lord Chelmsford's central column, Rorke's Drift was the true backup supply station. A trader's settlement, it occupied former stores and a yard near a river crossing on the Zululand boundary. Word of the massacre not many miles distant arrived by way of a few survivors riding exhausted horses. Most of the native troops at Rorke's Drift joined their headlong retreat. But the queen's soldiers, about eighty troops under two lieutenants, remained to defend their outpost. They had a little time to prepare. The store and adjoining converted hospital were pierced for rifle muzzles, and the yard was fortified with cornmeal sacks and biscuit boxes.

Soon after, an advance horde of about five hundred Zulus appeared from the east and ran whooping to the attack, concentrating on the hospital. Inside were six soldiers and about thirty patients. The Zulu swirled about the building, and soon made it perilously hot for the defenders by igniting the grass roof. Then the attackers broke through an entrance stuffed with meal bags. At a narrow inner doorway, Privates Henry Hook and John Williams faced them:

What were we to do? We were pinned like rats in a hole. Already the Zulus were fiercely trying to burst in through the doorway. The only way of escape was the wall itself—by making a hole big enough for a man to crawl through into an adjoining room, and so on until we got to our inmost entrenchment outside. Williams worked desperately at the wall with the navvy's pick, which I had been using to make some loopholes.

All this time the Zulus were trying to get into the room. Their assegais kept whizzing toward us, and one struck me in front of the helmet . . . I escaping with a scalp wound which did not trouble me much then. . . . A big Zulu sprang forward and seized my rifle; but I tore it free . . . and shot him point-blank. Time after time the Zulus gripped the muzzle and tried to tear the rifle from my grasp, and time after time I wrenched it back, because I had a better grip.

. . . Williams got all of the sick through the hole into the next room, except one, a soldier of the 24th named Conley, who could not move because of a broken leg. Watching for my chance, I dashed from the doorway, and grabbing Conley I pulled him after me through the hole. His leg got broken again, but there was no help for it. As soon as we left the room, the Zulus burst in with furious cries of disappointment and rage.

Private Hook earns his medals at Rorke's Drift.

The battle had begun about 4:30 P.M. and lasted nearly all night. Six times the Zulus overran the meal bags and biscuit boxes—and were wiped out by British bayonet charges. Toward dawn the fighting slackened, and in the morning light the Zulus withdrew. They left 351 corpses in the immediate area and total deaths were reckoned at about five hundred. The English had seventeen killed and ten wounded. Eleven Victoria Crosses, Britain's top military medal, were distributed among the defenders at Rorke's Drift, including a pair for Privates Hook and Williams.

In the aftermath, Lord Chelmsford well knew that he would be replaced, and pondered how to rescue his command reputation. He pressed on more vigilantly; in the end, the valiant, underweaponed Zulus could not stand against the technologically superior British. On July 4, 1879, before Ulindi, the Zulu capital, the famed quadruple line (two kneeling, two standing) redcoats' hollow-square battle formation mowed down thousands of spear-bearing Zulu attackers. Their king, Cetewayo, was afterward captured and the Zulu War ended, just as General Sir Garnet Wolsley came on to replace Lord Chelmsford.

Chelmsford had achieved personal satisfaction, but back in London he was not again offered a command. Chief Cetewayo was also brought to London. He became a celebrity there, and Queen Victoria invited him to tea. The Zulu War had cost Great Britain over thirteen hundred dead and wounded, and upset the South African budget.

The Zulu War taught the Transvaal Afrikaners that the English were not invincible. What the "Kaffirs" did, the Boers could do better. Also, now that the Zulu menace was finished, they could concentrate on Colonel Lanyon and his occupation force.

The spark that ignited Transvaal's revolution arose from a taxation grievance. The Transvaaler judged to be in arrears was a Bezuidenhout, a surname well remembered from the ghastly business at Slagter's Nek. The authorities tried to confiscate his wagon; in Transvaal this was akin to putting a citizen out of his home. The demonstrations of support were steered by leaders like Paul Kruger into general defiance of England and then to a proclamation of national independence.

It was only more Boer bluster, Colonel Lanyon wished to believe. But on December 20, 1880, an English reinforcement column of 235 troopers was intercepted by representatives of a two-hundred-man Boer commando and ordered to halt until replies had been received by their leaders from Colonel Lanyon in Pretoria on state affairs. English Colonel Anstruther, commanding, refused, saying he would follow his orders to march to Pretoria. Surrounding Boer marksmen quickly caused 120 casualties and picked off all the officers before the remnant surrendered. As soon as news of the one-sided battle spread, Boer units besieged all of the English troop installations in the land, preventing them from unified action. Future British military response would have to come from outside.

Sir George Colley was the general chosen for Transvaal's subordination. Upon his first field command, General Colley marched his little army of twelve hundred soldiers up from Natal to the border at a pass called Laing's Nek and found about two thousand Transvaal farmers under Piet Joubert on the ridge barring entry. They didn't look like an army—no uniforms or regular formation. They were widely spread and not standing to, either. Each lay peering out from some shelter. Not an army by European standards, but they all carried rifles and appeared resolute.

In correct close formation, British foot soldiers, assisted by a few cavalry, ascended to the attack, pausing properly to volley at the enemy. These fusillades were not effective, because the farmers were separated from each other and crouched behind cover. The English, panting, reached the sloping plateau on top and stared at an irregular line of rifle muzzles poking from behind rocks and earthworks. As the British fixed bayonets and were ordered into the charge, a long roll of Boer fire responded, and the English charge was blown away, most of its officers casualties. A sublieutenant directed their stumbling retreat. Of the 480 soldiers who climbed, 150 lay fallen at the top.

The English had lost the first organized battle. Only fourteen Boers died; their comrades, their nation, was infused with confidence. A Boer guerrillalike force got behind British lines and menaced the British supply routes. General Colley personally responded with three hundred troops, was nearly surrounded, and lost about half of his force. The wily and mobile Boers had only eight dead.

The war might have ended here; there was little support for it in England. But General Colley was in the same fix as Lord Chelmsford after his disaster. And Colley resolved to settle his problem the same way—to win this war before they took him away. Back at Laing's Nek, Majuba Hill rose steeply near the Boer line. A squad of Transvaalers daily occupied the summit for observation, but marched down each evening. General Colley decided to occupy the hilltop after dark. He succeeded on a Saturday night and was able to look down at the Boers' dawn Sunday breakfast.

Someone fired, and the distress below was certainly real as the foe scattered for cover and out of sight. But General Joubert and his tactician, Nicholas Smit, reacted coolly. Many of their sharpshooters were directed to begin and maintain firing at the British on the hill. The British, having gained great respect for enemy marksmanship, mostly ducked. Meanwhile, a few hundred intrepid Boers slipped around and, hoping to use their comrades' shooting as an artillery curtain, started up Majuba Hill.

The four hundred or so English soldiers huddled in hollows within the broad, shallow hilltop seemed not to have known this. There was a fumbled reaction and finally, a rout, after the Boer line popped over the enclosing ridge. The farmers hadn't run off after all. By 1:00 P.M. on February 27, 1881, nearly three hundred English were casualties or prisoners, of whom ninety-two were killed, including General Colley. One Boer was killed, five were wounded, one lay dying of wounds. Majuba Hill finished the war.

London's thought to reinforce its South African army and crush the Boer republic soon faded. Great Britain, in historian Oliver Ransford's phrase, "had grown bored with the stupid little war against a handful of farmers six thousand miles away," and Prime Minister Gladstone now generously moved toward peace without further bloodshed. Paul Kruger was cooperative, friendly, the English thought, now that he had received his reward. Transvaal was free—for the second time England had backed out of a Boer republic.

The political results of Majuba Hill were far-reaching. The British plan for confederation was shelved. Among many Afrikaners all over South Africa a fierce, chauvinistic nationalism had been kindled that would blaze forth throughout the future and divide the South African whites.

8

The Coming of the Boer War

Two years after Majuba Hill, Paul Kruger became president of Transvaal (South African Republic), and for about twenty years he continued as the Boer's chief of state. Given the contentious individuality of his countrymen, this alone was quite a political feat. He survived and thrived on balancing personal popularity with hard-nosed political purpose.

Certainly, he was the Boer's Boer. A man of his people, he was approaching sixty when he came into prominence. He had risen from the farm; had enjoyed acclaim as a commando leader; had become a national elder of the church; had journeyed to London and had negotiated on behalf of the Afrikaner nation; and the years had fulfilled him in land and substance (with a presidential salary of forty thousand dollars a year). But he had *not* changed. "Oom (uncle) Paul" remained his own man, strict and doctrinaire in honoring tradition, yet with a wily sense of diplomatic purpose and humor; living in an ordinary burgher's house in small-town Pretoria, approachable in his parlor by anyone, comfortable and homely as an old shoe.

But in the councils of the *volksraad* (congress), Kruger was transformed into a wild-eyed political champion of unflinching purpose and cunning. His principal governmental opponent over many years was Piet Joubert, who had defeated General Colley at Majuba Hill. An associate justified a setback to Joubert by Kruger in these words:

Old friend, it is like this: I do stand up against him, I know he is wrong and I tell him so; but first he argues with me, and if that is no good he gets into a rage and jumps around the room roaring at me like a wild beast . . . and if I do not give in, then he fetches out the Bible and . . . he even quotes that to help him out. And if all that fails he takes my hand and cries like a child and begs and prays me to give in. Say, old friend, who can resist a man like that?

The chief British power was Cecil Rhodes, who used his rising fortunes to propel himself all the way to become prime minister of the Cape Colony (1890). But it was as a private political operator that he scored his early success in confining the Afrikaner republics, especially Transvaal, to their official borders. The Boer escape valve had traditionally been any horizon, but Cecil Rhodes fenced them in permanently.

Not even spacious Transvaal now seemed big enough for its growing ranch-family population. The easiest outlet was to edge westward into Bechuanaland (now Botswana), and colonies were started in Stellaland and Goshen. Later on, thought the Kruger government comfortably, they could always expand by muscling into the northern wilderness beyond the Limpopo River, presently occupied by the fierce Zulu-like Matabele nation.

But they were checked right off in Bechuanaland, because their settlers pressed upon the "Great North Road" of Cecil Rhodes, where, someday, he expected his Cape-to-Cairo railway to run—on British soil, of course. So Rhodes sent agents to Stellaland and Goshen to buy up the allegiance of the scattered settlers, and shortly persuaded Great Britain to declare the territory a Crown protectorate (1885). Transvaal could not expand west.

Cecil Rhodes was also deeply drawn toward Matabeleland,

where he believed great gold fields lay awaiting discovery and British development. Rhodes wangled London's permission to establish a private imperial charter venture, Rhodesia, to operate north of Transvaal.

So Transvaal was denied its intended northern hinterland. The lowlands to the east, under Portuguese rule, were not attractive except as a vital rail exit to the Indian Ocean, which was achieved by Kruger (1895).

Despite his activities, Rhodes did not consider himself an enemy of the Boers. He insisted that he admired them. Certainly, he respected what he considered their practical attitude toward native relations, and their use of native labor. So he acted in restraint, preparing them for the union of all South African territories. In his political career in the Cape Colony, Rhodes successfully courted the support of the principal Afrikaner spokesman. He could foresee, from the growth of the Afrikaner Bond society, a long future of Afrikaner nationalism. Surely the Afrikaners must see the economic advantage of uniting under British rule, and in time the cultural benefit of becoming a united British nation, like Canada.

In 1886, the world's most massive gold strike occurred on the Witwatersrand (whitewater reef), about forty miles south of Pretoria. Gold prospecting of the pan-and-wash type had been done in Transvaal, with limited success, since the 1850s. Also, gold had been mined in quartzite seams as elsewhere. But the Rand gold was finely fused in a plunging series of rock strata later determined to be sixty miles long. Deep-shaft mining, expensive rock-crushing machinery, and gold-particle-collecting processes were required. Only people with capital could take advantage of it.

The nearest town with capital resources was Kimberley. Tycoon Joseph Benjamin Robinson hustled into the area and succeeded in buying or leasing from their proprietors likely Rand properties, because he spoke Afrikaans. Rhodes and Barnato also became prominent investors in the Rand bonanza. It is claimed that Rhodes amassed his greatest fortune here. Barnato made his headquarters in

Johannesburg—first a mining camp, then a town, soon a mighty city—which arose on the Witwatersrand. Year by year thousands of opportunists flocked into the enduring boomtown of Jo'burg. Nearly every nationality on earth had Rand emigres; many were Americans with mining experience. To the Transvaal Boers they were all birds of a feather—Uitlanders (outsiders).

Earlier, in the 1880s, Paul Kruger had welcomed the goldseekers. Transvaal's tax base was tottery as always, and the mine income of strangers could be safely taxed. After the big strike, the Rand mines easily supported the nation; and many Transvaalers, including President Kruger, profited handily in land speculations. Nevertheless, the situation, and its social and foreseen political effects, were very disturbing to the Afrikaners.

Johannesburg and the smaller Kimberley flourished, not rough and dangerous as boomtowns were on other continents, but still a place where money was worshiped and freely distributed upon pleasures of the flesh—wine, women, and song. Kimberley soon was absorbed into the relatively cosmopolitan Cape Colony, but Jo'burg remained under the rule of the ultraconservative *volksraad* in Pretoria, whose members devoutly believed that God had laid the gold in the Witwatersrand, but the Devil's children were digging it out and had built a Sodom atop their works.

Kruger rarely went into Johannesburg (only forty miles away), and when he did so he seemed distracted by its coarse hurly-burly and English foreignness. Since the president resolutely refused to speak English (but somewhat tolerated understanding it), communication was variable, and Kruger often seemed stiff and rude. He was offended when someone invited him to a horse race (gambling!), and shot back that he didn't have to go to a race to know that one horse could run faster than another. He disapproved of the numerous taverns (drink!), was further put off by their hospitable hostesses, and the lack of a color bar in many of the humbler dives.

The pious Boers erected one effective barrier against what they considered an Uitlander cesspool. The strangers were denied Transvaal citizenship (the vote) until they had been residents for fourteen years. This wasn't an active campaign to push out the foreigners—not when they paid such handsome taxes! As for the fleshpots of Jo'burg—let 'em stew in them; as non-Calvinists, they were believed predestined to hell anyway.

The Randlords, their advisers, engineers, and skilled artisans were thus placed into practically the same class as the black workers. By the Afrikaner code, you saw to it that they worked profitably, but on no account did you mingle with them in society or politics. In the Rand mines, the ratio was about one (skilled) white to seven blacks. White nonprofessional salaries averaged $115 per month; blacks earned $15 with board (1889).

Then, a mine operator's cartel was able to depress mine wages about twenty-five percent. When this caused the native labor sources to wane, Transvaal increased the supply again by laying a head tax on nonworkers that most couldn't afford.

The Uitlanders felt their host nation was sadly out of date by all social and economic standards in the real world of the late nineteenth century. They bombarded Pretoria with petitions for improvements and, finding this unavailing, itched to take over the national government. Here they were blocked by the bar against their vote. The *volksraad,* too contentious and old-fashioned for possible efficiency, rejected most of the suggestions from Johannesburg for selfish or moral reasons. And their appointed officials on the Rand were decidedly not up to the pace of modern times.

Pressures built up. Rustic inefficiency wasn't picturesque when it blocked profits. The Randlords formed a powerful political action committee, the Transvaal National Union. As a concession, the Afrikaaners reduced residence for citizenship to ten years. Beyond this the president stood rock-firm:

> *If the greater part of the people consist of loyal citizens who are fully enfranchised, then a small number of newcomers cannot do any harm. But if the latter are in the majority, then the old population is afraid of sharing their rights with them and so giving away their power. . . .*

See that flag? If I grant the franchises, I may as well pull it down.

Probably "Oom Paul" felt the danger most keenly in the social sector. The traditional Boer life-style would be soiled amid Uitlander ways; their children would become heathens!

"Foreigners and outcasts in a strange land," chorused the Randlord's complaint, "paying taxes for the support of the state, but denied any share in the administration or apportionment of them." Change must be forced, then. When the mining tycoons imagined controlling Transvaal, they did not necessarily add British rule. They might be better off as a corporate gold nation, wheeling and dealing around the world. For one thing, they found the native policies of the Boers, with their racist views on labor, good for profits.

The super-Randlord, Cecil Rhodes, looked beyond a capitalist gold state. His thrust was always toward more power; his eye on a South Africa bound together under British rule. For the second time in twenty years, Transvaal was viewed as the stickiest part of the federation process. Rhodes's idea was to goad the frustrated Johannesburgers into revolution and boost them from outside with his own private army from Rhodesia. The inefficient Kruger regime would shortly collapse, and Afrikaners elsewhere in South Africa would more readily turn toward Rhodes's own Anglo-Boer coalition.

The plan was patently in the British interest, and a bold activist, Joseph Chamberlain, was now the Colonial Office secretary. Because of treaty stipulations made with the South African Republic after Majuba Hill, Britain needed to appear clean-handed in the adventure. Once the Johannesburg rebels wrenched control, then the British could move in on the plea of "protecting lives and property of British subjects." Still, it would have been much better if the Rand rebels did it all themselves. So the affair had to be coordinated between the Rand conspirators and the outside force, and that force *not* launched unless assured of success.

In effect, Rhodes had been counseled by Chamberlain to go ahead with his revolution when certain of success, and with his own resources. That suited Rhodes, but it was a poor plan strategically for Rhodes's army to come straight down from the north. The best way in was from the western Bechuanaland border. Helpfully, London ceded a strip of their Bechuanaland protectorate to Rhodes's British South Africa Company (Rhodesia) in exchange for Rhodes's promise that the new Transvaal would be British.

Cecil Rhodes worked out the details of the Transvaal destabilization. He coached the leader of the Uitlanders' political National Union, Charles Leonard, and paid for and arranged secret arms shipments into Johannesburg. Sentiment for revolt was secretly whipped up there, but several of the major mining companies never went in with the plotters.

Rhodes's best friend, Dr. Leander Starr Jameson, was the man in charge of the private army that would rush in to assist the Uitlander revolt. He was a Rhodes loyalist and shared his mentor's enthusiasms and dreams. The militant doctor possessed a letter of appeal signed by the rebel Randlords but not dated; it was his invitation to invade Johannesburg and Pretoria. Jameson had a low opinion of the Transvaalers and he had confidence in his weapons. The machine gun (Maxim) had been invented; Jameson had eight Maxims, the Boers, zero.

As December came on, the adventure turned sour. Jameson, supposed to raise fifteen hundred men, could find only five hundred. Paul Kruger, in a public forum, replied to a questioner: "I am often asked about a threatened rising, and I say, wait until the time comes. Take the tortoise; if you want to kill it you must wait until it puts out its head, then you can cut it off." Near the date, Charles Leonard, the Rand rebel organizer, decided there was insufficient enthusiasm and manpower for a revolution and signaled for cancellation of the coup attempt. He appealed to Kruger for a fresh try to settle Uitlander grievances and was answered affirmatively.

Letters, telegrams, and personally delivered messages failed to deter Dr. Leander Starr Jameson. He waited to hear from his master, who remained silent, implying to Jameson that he should go ahead. Cecil Rhodes claimed then and afterward that he had done his best to stop Dr. Jameson; but facts don't bear this out. Rhodes had heard from Joseph Chamberlain in London that a developing crisis with the United States (over Venezuela) would soon require all British attention. Rhodes, on his own, allowed the Transvaal coup to continue.

On Sunday evening, December 29, 1895, Jameson's small but well-armed force entered Transvaal. Each trooper carried an extra rifle to hand to a Rand rebel down the road. Relying on supposed food caches ahead, the force carried only a day's ration. The expedition began with a botch. A patrol sent to cut Transvaal's telegraph line became drunk and cut a farmer's fence wire instead. Jameson's progress was watched by the Transvaalers, but they lay well back, assembling commandos west of Johannesburg.

When the word of Jameson's "approach" reached Johannesburg, an indecisive revolt occurred. That is, the city was taken over by the capitalists, but no attempt to spread beyond the city was made. Kruger prudently withdrew his police without firing a shot.

Jameson bogged down. Messengers repeatedly arrived: from the Boers inquiring his intent, then telling him to go back; from Sir Hercules Robinson, the high commissioner in Capetown, ordering them back. But their reply was that they were too hungry—food and friends were not far ahead. The only party they met, one hundred miles or so into Transvaal, was the citizen commandos.

Jameson had experienced officers. They set up the Maxims and portable artillery. Formed up and blazing away, the troopers charged the Boer position—and found it empty! The Boers at the sides and rear used their guns effectively. Surrounded, exhausted, the troopers surrendered, and that was the end of the Jameson Raid. On the evening of January 2, over four hundred Rhodesians were locked up in Pretoria's jail. Seventeen of the expedition had been killed, fifty-six wounded.

Cecil Rhodes now entered the blackest period of his life. He resigned immediately as premier of the Cape Colony. Urged by

Afrikaner political ally Jan Hofmeyr to repudiate the errant doctor, Rhodes replied: "Well, you see, Jameson has been such an old friend, of course I cannot do it." Hofmeyr's friendship ceased, and from then onward the split between Afrikaner and Englishman became permanent everywhere. Rhodes was finished as a Cape politician, but remained a wealthy power broker to the end.

Early on, Transvaal's government received a guileful telegram from Joseph Chamberlain in London, reading in part: "Regret to hear of Jameson's actions. . . . Can I cooperate further in this emergency . . . ?"

Kruger informed the rebels in Johannesburg that he was prepared to execute Dr. Jameson and his followers unless they promptly surrendered. They promptly did so. Now the jail was further jammed with millionaire Uitlander revolutionaries. In the exercise yard, the two captured factions railed at each other.

By a masterful stroke Kruger got rid of Jameson and his raiders by turning them over to Great Britain for trial and punishment. Even though the English had backed the plot, at least in its planning, they now had to go through the motions of punishing *themselves*. In England, the Raid leaders were tried and found guilty of carrying out warlike actions against a friendly nation. Prison sentences of up to fifteen months were handed down, some of which were served.

Though Cecil Rhodes soon sailed to England "to face the music," he wound up only reprimanded. British public opinion in the 1890s was strongly proimperialist, and sympathy for underdog Transvaal faded when Germany blunderingly supported the Boers. Rhodes, in a later visit, audaciously told Kaiser Wilhelm:

> *You see I was a naughty boy and you tried to whip me. Now my people were quite ready to whip me for being a naughty boy, but directly you did it, they said, 'No, if this is anybody's business, it is ours.' The result was that your Majesty got yourself very much disliked by the English people, and I never got whipped at all.*

Meanwhile Kruger and the *volksraad* charged the captive Rand-lords and their accomplices, sixty-five in all, with high treason. Dr. Jameson had failed to destroy his letter of invitation, and the court tended to concentrate upon four jailed signers of it, including Cecil's brother, Colonel Frank Rhodes.

Tough sentences were handed down to all, including death by hanging for four. It was Kruger's bluff again. He had no intent to provide martyrs to the British cause. But he wished to underline the gravity of the offense for future reference and to squeeze out all he could in benefits for Transvaal over several months of suspense. Eventually, it cost Cecil Rhodes over $2 million to free his friends.

So the affair ended; nothing was settled. Actually, the confrontation to come had been set by the British when they learned the Transvaal gold ores were tremendous in extent. In London and Uitlander South Africa it was decided that Transvaal must be absorbed before its gold would make it so powerful it could absorb the rest of South Africa.

A new cool, pragmatic South African high commissioner, Sir Alfred Milner, was sent down from Britain (1898). He was single-minded: "The case for intervention is overwhelming. . . . The spectacle of thousands of British subjects kept permanently in the position of helots, constantly chafing under undoubted grievances and calling vainly to her majesty's government for redress, steadily undermines the influence and reputation of Great Britain and respect for British government."

Milner hoped that a less-rigid politician would come into power in Transvaal, but the 1898 presidential election there returned the aged "Oom Paul." Of Milner, Kruger observed in his memoirs: "Mr. Chamberlain appointed Sir Alfred Milner with a view to driving matters in South Africa to extremes."

The inflexibility of Britain's purpose impressed Kruger and Transvaal. They believed they must submit or fight. Transvaal made a military alliance with its sister Boer republic, the Orange Free State. Kruger purchased armaments and attempted to arrange alliances with European powers like Germany and France. If war was inevitable, as the Boers decided it to be, it was important to strike before Britain had loaded South Africa with armies.

On October 11, 1899, the two little Afrikaner republics declared war upon the mightiest imperial nation on earth at that time. President Kruger told an American newspaper: "The republics are determined, if they must belong to England, that a price will be paid that will stagger humanity."

9

To a Bitter End

The war aims of the Boer War adversaries could be stated thus: Great Britain was set to extinguish the political independence of the two Afrikaner republics; Transvaal and the Orange Free State vowed, whatever else, to maintain their national freedom. A burgher of Pretoria understood it in everyday terms: "In the future I must take off my hat to an Englishman, or he must take off his hat to me."

Like many wars, this one opened amid false assumptions on both sides. The English, as usual, underestimated the enemy. The Boers would fight neither long nor hard, it was believed, and the South African affair would be gloriously completed by Christmas. For their part, the Boers wished desperately to believe that a strong demonstration of resistance would be enough. If the republics showed that they meant business, Britain would back off (as they had after Majuba Hill). Kruger and company counted, too, on world opinion and hoped for outside political and military support.

In September 1899, as the grass greened in the high veld springtime, the Boer republics mobilized their horseback citizen armies. All males sixteen to sixty were subject to military service. They were joined by numerous volunteers both below and above the specified ages. In reporting to his local commando, the recruit was required to provide a riding horse, saddle and bridle, a weapon, thirty bullets,

caps, and one-half pound of gunpowder. Also he had to bring sufficient food, dried salted meat and biscuits, to sustain himself during
the first eight days of his national service.

As many commandos as possible were outfitted with the fine new
Mauser military rifles imported from Germany. This very accurate

No generation gap: a family unit in the Boer War.

weapon in skilled Afrikaner hands killed at distances up to a mile. The horseback commandos moved at four times the pace of the opposing infantry, over territory they knew far better than did the foe. Commandos were loose in formation and very adaptive to local opportunities. But a related drawback was their lack of discipline. They were independent soldiers who joined, left, and rejoined the war to suit their family responsibilities.

In September, there were only a few thousand English troops in South Africa, and the republics' advantage was at least four to one. Jan C. Smuts, President Kruger's brilliant young man, devised a plan: Slash down into Natal, capture Durban! Invade the Cape Colony, too, and probably many of the Afrikaners there would rise in revolt. They might even take Capetown; then the English troop fleets could not land. Surely reason and peace would follow. On September 9, the Boers knew that troop ships were sailing south. But President Marthinus Steyn of the Orange Free State was reluctant to go to war except as the last choice, and another month passed before he agreed with Kruger to a joint war declaration.

In Britain the conflict has since become known as "the last gentlemen's war," that is, where opportunity for personal glory—in a cavalry charge, or leading a company of foot with saber outstretched, beckoned.

By tacit agreement this was a white man's war. The Boers would scarcely arm their natives, of course; but Britain also refrained from using its crack Indian Army. The Imperialists and the Chosen People fought in racial purity.

When in mid-October the commandos finally lashed out, they still might have done it according to plan, though their manpower margin was declining as ships docked and English regiments marched off. But instead, the Afrikaner armies halted just beyond their national boundaries to besiege three enemy junction towns of importance: Mafeking, to the west of Transvaal; Kimberley, to the southwest of the Orange Free State; and Ladysmith, south of the Orange Free State in British Natal. When Cecil Rhodes heard of the Boers' approach, he managed to board the last train *into*

Kimberley, thereby becoming a famous hostage whom England must rescue.

The Boers' offense was thus essentially a defense. They were doing their demonstration and preparing to repulse the English when *they* came up toward the beleaguered towns. The separate forces of the British commanding general, Sir Redvers Buller (afterward "Sir Reverse"), got off to a terrible start. Blind in luck, tactics, knowledge, maps, and coordination, they stumbled courageously into bloody defeats. There was confusion; and repeated instances of English soldiers falling under the fire of their own artillery.

In mid-December's "Black Week," Great Britain sustained three stinging reverses. At Colenso in Natal, where Buller personally commanded, the brigade sent to attack a flank got lost and suffered severe casualties. Then the officer in charge of the precious artillery just delivered from England dragged the pieces out way ahead of the center of English infantry, too far into the killing zone of the Boers' Mauser rifles. Shortly, one-third of the gunners became casualties, along with the horses. The shocked remainder of artillerymen huddled in the scant cover of a shallow ravine. The cannons were anyone's war booty.

Buller, in effect, decided to call off his attack to concentrate on retrieving his guns from no-man's-land. His soldiers got back only two of the ten cannons; and the suicidal rescue attempts caused the watching Boer general, Louis Botha, human agony amid tactical exultation:

> *All our people were watching: it was a terrible thing to see, like looking down at a play from the gallery. When the teams and men were shot down, just swept away by fire . . . and when we saw another lot of men and more teams dash to work to save the guns we held our breath; it was madness; nothing could live there. Then came another lot, and another and another . . . I was sick with horror that such bravery should be so useless. God, I turned away and could not look; and yet I had to look again. It was too wonderful.*

The British casualties at Colenso that day were twelve hundred. General Buller was removed from overall command by the War Office in London.

For Britain, this made three Majuba Hill–style losses in a week! But soon the high hopes of Presidents Kruger and Steyn cooled as they became aware of their mistake in believing the British would give way. No, not so long as High Commissioner Alfred Milner served in South Africa. Unconditional surrender remained his blunt bottom line, and London concurred. More troops were raked together to be sent south. An appeal for volunteers went out in Britain and overseas in the Empire.

From the world the Afrikaners gathered admiration, but not a single supportive governmental action. In England, where it counted, the pro-Boer opposition was loud but lacked political punch. The Boers were doomed and would be ground down in the New Year. Even the German Kaiser Wilhelm wrote to support his English relative, Queen Victoria. He advised her to send down Britain's top military heroes, Lord Roberts and Lord Kitchener; and, coincidentally, that is what the War Office did. Lord Roberts's only son had been killed in the ghastly gun-retrieval business at Colenso.

English newspapers ignored the losses and concentrated on what was occurring in the three besieged towns, which all pluckily held out. It was touch and go at Ladysmith, which the Boer armies really wanted as a key to Natal. At Kimberley, Cecil Rhodes's pronouncements and checkbook won the day; but Mafeking was the crowd pleaser, because it was the littlest and longest beset—and featured Colonel Robert Baden-Powell, master of the art of carrying on a "gentlemen's war."

There is disagreement about Baden-Powell's grasp of war strategy. The colonel is criticized after the fact for inviting the siege at the desolate high veld railroad town of Mafeking (pronounced Mahfykin) when he might have diverted more enemy troops by raids through northern Transvaal. But the English commander's dash, pluck, and wit in directing his men through 217 days of siege caught the attention, then the admiration of the British public.

Colonel Robert Baden-Powell: He knew how to manipulate a "gentlemen's war."

That four prominent English war correspondents shared the long, mostly uneventful siege certainly helped Baden-Powell's popularization. They wished to write of something beside the boredom and picked up on the publicity-conscious commanding officer.

That Mafeking was allowed to thrive as a national symbol of defiance was the doing of the Boers. At the start, commandos totaling six thousand or more ranged outside Baden-Powell's well arranged and dug-in force of about one thousand. Though they were mostly pick-up "irregulars," the colonel had capable officers on his staff.

After the English had barely beaten back the first serious attack, surprisingly the enemy did not try again. It was reported that President Kruger had remarked that Mafeking was not worth more than fifty casualties. So most of the Boer troops went away, down south, where the action was hot and heavy; Mafeking's strategic purpose of keeping the Boer army tied up was defeated. But its publicity value would grow and grow.

The remaining troops, about two thousand, lapsed into a sitzkrieg (sitting war), creating a gentlemen's climate for both sides. Those Boers who lingered were local men. Without much trouble, they could get away to work on their farms as necessary. A trip to the safe edge of the siege positions became a kind of picnic outing for Afrikaner families. Papa at the front might arrange that Mama pull the cannon lanyard to hurl a shell into English Mafeking.

The Boers expected to pound and starve the enemy enclave into surrender. They dragged up a huge cannon recently delivered from France. "Old Creaky," as the English dubbed it, hurled ninety-four-pound projectiles, about fifteen hundred of them, into Mafeking during the siege, but with little effect; perhaps one in a hundred caused injury or death. The town was spread out, its populace had dug numerous shelters, and the mostly earthen-walled dwellings, when hit, smothered the explosion.

The commanders wrote objectively or complainingly to each other very often. The Boers' General Cronje, believing the Englishmen to be shell-shocked, early on requested the English surrender "to avoid further bloodshed." Baden-Powell, who up to that time had counted just two bombardment casualties—a hen killed outright, and a dog died of wounds—impudently responded, "But we haven't had any yet." However, the shelling was an unfriendly gesture, he felt, and if continued might amount to "a declaration of war."

The English colonel tried to baffle the Boers by setting stovepipes as cannons, stringing fake barbed wire, and sending his men out daily to bury bogus land mines. Other tricks tried out during the months of sitzkrieg included casting grenades into enemy positions with a fishing rod. Meanwhile, Baden-Powell's natural talents as a showman bolstered the town's morale by an amazing variety of fun and games: cricket, polo, feasts, plays, music variety shows, and dances. And, yes, at a ball, the officers in dress uniform had to depart for an hour or so to deal with a small Boer raid. Dreary, isolated Mafeking was never so festive as during its siege.

The Boers piously observed Sundays as a day of rest, a gift happily accepted by Mafeking's gentlemen. Each side prayed to God for victory, and then the English played. Commandant J. P. Snijman, a strict Boer who took over the sitzkrieg, threatened to shell the sacrilege of cricket and polo matches on Sunday, and for a while Baden-Powell put on indoor Sunday entertainments.

MAY XMAS FIND YOU GLAD AND WELL, IN SPITE OF KRUGER'S SHOT AND SHELL. Below this jaunty salutation, the Mafeking Hotel holiday menu bulged with the following items: oyster patties, smoked calves tongue, roast fowl, baron of beef, suckling pig and apple sauce, roast saddle of mutton, Yorkshire puddings, and mince pies. Some starvation siege! It was a good example of Baden-Powell's motto. Be prepared. (He founded the international Boy Scout movement in later years.) A soldier showing off to a girlfriend on Christmas Day accidentally set off a few machine-gun rounds toward Boerland. Immediately a messenger set out to deliver an apology.

But at dawn of the day after Christmas, the colonel's gentlemen and troops attacked an enemy stronghold and were bloodily repulsed. Anguished, Baden-Powell immediately sent out a flag of truce, and the Boer soldiers responded by emerging from their bastion to help tend the English wounded, as Victorian courtesies were exchanged all around. English casualties were fifty, including twenty-four dead, versus three killed defenders. The Boers did not return an attack, and the sitzkrieg resumed.

To the southward, where war was hellish all of the time, in the new year the tide of battle turned against the Boers. Lord Roberts pushed on to capture the Orange Free State capital of Bloemfontein (March 1900). Both Ladysmith and Kimberley had been rescued from encirclement in February. It did not appear that the Boer armies could stand against the reinforced British in set battles. Transvaal would soon be invaded, Johannesburg and Pretoria captured, with the Kruger government in flight.

But, British public attention became riveted on brave little Mafeking, now six months into its siege. When would it be relieved? Lord Roberts ("Bobs") had properly considered it a sideshow and followed other priorities. By now they were thought to be starving. Horse sausage and husk porridge were reported dining staples; barbecued locusts had been tried; and whiskey prices were out of sight. But Colonel Baden-Powell was better stocked than was known outside. Finally, Kruger ordered an all-out attack on Mafeking, and sent Sarel Eloff, one of his thirty-five fighting grandsons, to lead it. The Boers managed a nighttime penetration of the town, but then they failed. On May 17, 1900, Mafeking was finally relieved, as London declared a hysterical holiday.

It seemed that the conflict had to be over; there was a positive response to Lord Roberts's offer of amnesty by pledging allegiance to new British rule. But the Boer Republic's presidents and military commandants in council in east Transvaal's backlands refused to give in. They vowed to go on as freedom fighters while Kruger sailed to Europe to make a personal appeal for foreign aid. The commandos would be put to their most natural use in hit-and-run guerrilla warfare. Meanwhile, elderly Lord "Bobs" returned home in triumph, leaving Lord Kitchener to mop up. Again, Christmas 1900 seemed, but was not, the date when victory would be total.

The decision to fight on placed the Afrikaner people, especially those near British stations, between a rock and a hard place. They were divided into those who had signed with the English, "handsuppers," or guerrilla partisans, "bitterenders." Since the commandos determined to live off the land, and the British wanted to prevent that, farmers were attacked from both sides. The commando foragers demanded supplies and military cooperation. The English confiscated all of his goods and burned his farm buildings if they suspected he supplied the commandos. The last two years of the Boer War fell most terribly upon the civilian population.

Lord Horatio Herbert Kitchener, thirty-six, with his piercing glance and brisk, cold manner, made a fearsome first impression. His military reputation had recently peaked in harsh actions against militant Arab sects in the Sudan; but Lord Kitchener was not a military sadist. He did not favor extermination of the Boers (but rather expected they'd be transported somewhere else afterward). Kitchener was as cruel and extreme as necessary in combating guerrilla forces, the most frustrating action a standard army fights.

To protect lines of communication and supply, in particular the railroads, Kitchener undertook the construction of about eight thousand linked, fortified blockhouses. He also erected thousands of miles of barbed wire to try to pen commandos within specific areas to be swept up by British troops. But the sweeps were not usually successful, as sly and courageous Boer generals—Botha, de la Rey, de Wet, Hertzog, Smuts—always managed to get away to fight again, to sting the English at their weakest points. Indeed the guerrilla war included deep, daring raids into the Cape Colony. The years 1900 and 1901 passed without conclusive British victories, though the commandos became pared down and worn threadbare. About sixteen thousand freedom fighters remained active—the best of breed, lean, savvy, and tough. The British troop investment swelled to 220,000.

The most controversial of Kitchener policies was the establish-

"Ordeal by Fire": A heroic view of "the last gentlemen's war."

ment of civilian "concentration camps." Young Winston Churchill was a Boer War newspaper correspondent, and in later years wrote in overview:

> *This long-drawn-out struggle bred shocking evils. The roving enemy wore no uniforms of their own; they mingled with the population, lodged and were succoured in farmhouses whose owners had taken the oath of neutrality, and sprang into being, now here, now there, to make some formidable and bloody attack upon an unwary column or isolated post. To cope with all this the British military authorities found it necessary to clear whole districts of their inhabitants and gather the population into concentration camps. As the rail-*

ways were continually cut, it was difficult to supply these camps with all the necessaries of life. Disease broke out, and several thousands of women and children died.

By the end of 1901, the English-held railroads had become ringed by forty-seven camps stuffed with 117,000 civilians, mostly women and children. Initially the English believed that permanent family separation would draw in substantial numbers of guerrillas, but once more the Uitlanders misjudged Boer tenacity. Actually, at the start, many commando soldiers were relieved that their families were out of the dangerous no-man's-land and were "safe" in British hands.

The Boers remained on the defensive after the war's opening months.

The concentration camps were not punishment facilities. They were tented holding depots modeled on current English military encampments. An accumulation of circumstances led to disaster in the camps: The inmates arrived exhausted from privations on the veld. They were not revived by the dreary, nonnutritious camp food, and were not able to resist rampant infectious diseases. Little common sense (boiling of water was unthought of) was applied by either the camp overseers or the inmates in coping with typhoid, diphtheria, and a combined outbreak of measles and pneumonia. Antibiotics did not exist.

The toll rose far beyond Mr. Churchill's "several thousands." In fact, about twenty-eight thousand persons died of disease in the concentration camps (seven times the number of Boer military dead) and *twenty-two thousand were children.* In October 1901, a camp child's risk of death was fifty-fifty. Thereafter, due largely to the efforts of English gentlewoman Emily Hobhouse and associates, who advocated good hygiene, the death rate declined sharply (from three thousand in October to two hundred in May 1902, when the war ended).

There were other camps not so well publicized. Perhaps the worst were the hovels where the English refugees from the Boer republics lived almost as street people in the slums of Durban. Also, 116,000 displaced blacks lived in concentration camps, and 14,000 of them died there. Black sufferings in the war-torn veld are a hidden statistic of a white man's war.

The war was "white" only on the trigger finger. Blacks dug the trenches, piled the fortifications, hauled supplies, erected blockhouses, strung barbed wire, and even dug the graves for fallen whites. The black presence was essential to conduct of the war on both sides. Blacks working for the British might receive prime wartime wages, or higher prices for their agricultural produce; but the Boers pushed labor-by-the-whip, unpaid except for some hope of secondary battlefield spoils. Black farmers taking over vacated Boer lands surely faced trouble when the veterans returned. Yet they at least for a while sampled the ideal of equality with the whites. But by the peace agreement that finally ended the war, the black majority population was headed onto a course of segregation and rights denial that led eventually to the rage of Soweto.

By May of 1902, the resisting Boers' military and civilian position had eroded to the point where the field commandants decided that it was time to end the war and win the peace—not necessarily such a farfetched goal, considering how war-weary the British were. Also, there was opportunity for new leadership as former personalities left politics. Aged Paul Kruger had failed in his personal European pleas and would not return again to South Africa, but died in 1904, an exile in Switzerland. Cecil Rhodes's heart failed and he died at forty-nine. A peace conference was warily convened, first in British Pretoria, then at a conference of sixty Boer leaders at Vereeniging, in the hinterland.

The stern civilian commissioner, Sir Alfred Milner, who yearned to and would rebuild South Africa according to his and London's blueprint, still favored unconditional surrender. In other parleys he had been a blunt take-it-or-leave-it "negotiator." But here this hard-liner was upstaged by a general in a hurry. Lord Kitchener was eager to be on his way to more attractive challenges. He became an avid negotiator and arranged for both sides to put forth proposals and then argue themselves into compromise.

The principal points in the Kitchener-Boer-generated peace were these: All Boers were to lay down their weapons and swear allegiance to the British monarch, now Edward VII, marking the end of Afrikaner political independence. Then property ownership would be restored to prewar conditions and no punishing reparation bill paid. Indeed, Britain agreed to loan $15 million in reconstruction funding for individuals. Boer social customs would be safeguarded, their Afrikaans language would be made official in courts and schools.

Local self-government was promised soon. But would the blacks receive limited civil rights as in the Cape Colony? Technically, this decision was postponed until Transvaal and the Orange Free State were self-governing; effectively, the Afrikaners would never then vote for black civil rights. This "Clause Nine" was a major English political blunder. It guaranteed eventual supremacy for the faster-growing Boer population, which would outnumber English South Africans in a few decades. Had the British insisted on a limited black franchise, expanding it over the years, a natural political alliance might have kept the Afrikaners as a loyal minority.

The Anglo-Boer War ended (May 31, 1902) and the butcher presented the bill: (figures approximate) 450,000 British soldiers served (top strength 230,000), of whom 22,000 died—6,000 in action, 16,000 of disease; 55,000 Boer soldiers served (top strength 35,000) and 34,000 Boers died—4,000 in action, most of the remainder civilians, including 22,000 children. More than 30,000 farmhouses were destroyed, most deliberately torched. Deep animosity lingered between the handsuppers and the bitterenders. A commando veteran willingly shook the hand of the British soldier who disarmed him; but back home he refused for twenty years and more to speak to his handsupper neighbor.

All the future names of prominence in South African politics would be Afrikaner. Commando generals, notably Louis Botha and Jan C. Smuts, would rule in the British dominion for forty years.

10

The White Man on Top

Back in 1842, when Dr. Philip's practical Christian idealism motivated English policy and his missionary advocates of native civil rights were still powerful in the field, Colonial Secretary Lord Stanley promised that in South Africa: "There shall not be in the eye of the law any distinction of colour, origin, race or creed; but that protection of the law, in letter and substance, shall be extended impartially to all alike." And it became promisingly so in the Cape Colony, even to the extent that the Cape Coloured populace were granted the vote on a par with English and Boer citizens.

But a half-century later, approximately half of expanded South Africa was ruled by the Boers, whose outlook on native entitlements was frankly bleak:

> *As to the Native Question, the Briton, even if he be haughty, believes that the coloured man is a human being, and British law treats him as such. The Boer looks upon him, even if Christianized, civilized, and educated, as a mere animal, and acts accordingly, often treating him kindly as one does a domestic animal, but as often treating him brutally without compunction, and ridiculing the very idea of his having a claim to the same civil, legal, political, and religious rights as the white man.*

So it was to be expected that, when the time came that the two white tribes fought each other furiously for years, the blacks helped the British wherever they could. And after the Boers surrendered their arms and nationhood to the English, the blacks expected to receive their reward. They expected the English to supervise Boer cultural-rights practices. However, black South Africans became the first to realize that in practice the Afrikaners had come out on top after all. In 1906 an educated black spokesman mourned that "the black races in these colonies feel today that their last state is worse than their first."

Expediency, not steadfastness, had come to characterize imperial policy. This war had already cost the British nearly $2 billion, a shocking and unexpected sum. South Africa must be made a paying property: First peace, and afterward a cooperative local Afrikaner government. So when Boer obstinacy on racial matters threatened the treaty, Britain easily sold out black civil rights in Transvaal and the Orange Free State. Next, Lord Milner's urge was to get the Rand gold mines producing again. Profits were to be maximized, and an easy measure was to reduce native wages to one-half of the prewar rate of about ten dollars a month (including board).

The English found out they had overdone. Half-pay was no incentive, and recruitment of black labor lagged badly. Then Milner went overseas and recruited (1904–1906) up to fifty thousand Chinese contract laborers, the cheapest miners of all. The Chinese generally worked well enough, but most were gamblers who tried to gain their fortunes in reckless fashion. Deep losers who could not pay up were mutilated or murdered by their Chinese creditors, and some deadbeats chose suicide.

The addition of still another "heathen" race really put local Afrikaner noses out of joint. When occasionally the Chinese would escape their compounds with the intent to walk home, there was dither in the countryside as if man-eating lions were prowling near. It was a common practice of Afrikaner bosses—flogging—that upset Milner's plans.

"*We need workers at the mines.*"

The Conservative party in the English Parliament, war-weary and beset by the Liberal party that had opposed the late war, toppled from rule when scare headlines and speeches proclaimed that the Conservative government looked aside while capitalists enslaved Chinese and were whipping and working them to death in the Rand gold mines. Lord Milner's African rule ended, and every last Chinese was transported home (as were the ashes of the Orientals who died, each packed neatly in a tea box). The Randlords jiggled the wage rate enough to attract the normal influx of native laborers, then pondered whether they could get away with training them for mid-level mine jobs. The blacks would, of course, work far more cheaply than the present semiskilled white labor.

During a dozen years following the Boer War, the white power structure was harassed unceasingly by the civil-rights pleas of the other imported Asian race residing in South Africa. Natal's sugar plantations, unable to attract native labor, had from the 1860s imported Indians with ten-year labor contracts; this same deal was employed by the coal industry. The Indian population worked out well for plantation managers and mine bosses, but the other citizens of predominantly English Natal weren't happy. The Indians offended Britons by their alien culture and their proud persistence in keeping to it.

Muslim Indians with a bit of investment capital began immigrating into Natal, ostensibly to become small businessmen trading with the Indian community, which was expanding, as many did not return to India at contract expiration. However, their business ability easily spread them into the white marketplace.

The merchant immigrants lived very frugally; the whites thought they lived squalidly. Polygamy fostered large families, who labored from childhood in the family business. This, plus marketing skill, caused them to overwhelm neighborhood white competition. The white housewife, despite her anti-Indian prejudice, still favored trading at "my Arab's," because his price was always right. Lower overhead allowed price undercutting that the white storekeeper could not meet.

When "Arab" enterprise had spread into Transvaal, in 1899 the British *Johannesburg Star* newspaper editorialized:

> *Apart from the question of his loathsome habits, the [Indian] is not an immigrant to be encouraged. He lowers the standard of comfort and closes the avenues to prosperity to the European trader. Economically, he is of no advantage to the country he visits—for, be it remembered that he does not settle. He accumulates money by virtue of the wretchedness in which he lives—a wretchedness constituting a terrible danger to the rest of the community—and he takes 80% of that money back again to Asia.*

So why didn't South Africa deport the unwanted Indian merchants and stop others from coming? Because they were not foreigners, like the Chinese laborers. The Indians were citizens of the British Empire on a par with South Africans. The Indian government interested itself in the legal welfare of its emigrants, and the British government was thereby obliged to appear virtuous.

Exclusion would have to be finagled without mentioning "Indians" in the punitive regulations: licensing laws, poll taxes, deportation outlets, immigration hurdles. Ultrawhite Australia had a literacy requirement that allowed the immigration official to test an unwanted immigrant in a European language of Australian choice—one the officer was certain the applicant did not know—and then to exclude the fellow! The failure of a similar South African law was caused by one man.

In 1893, a twenty-four-year-old English-educated Indian lawyer stepped off a ship at Durban harbor. Mohandas K. Gandhi's purpose was to argue a civil case involving the two countries, then return to India. But he became so passionately committed to the Natal Indian's worsening civil plight that he stayed in South Africa twenty-one years, advocating their cause.

Though Gandhi spent time skillfully arguing cases in the courts, his aim was to publicize the poor treatment of the Indians. His speeches and writings were widely read, and his position of leadership was strengthened by examples of civil disobedience that amazed and discomfited his white antagonists.

Four groups were involved in the decades of civil-rights maneuvering: Gandhi's Indian minority; the provincial and national South African government; the government of India; and the British government. The local government was solidly anti-Indian. India was sympathetic to its emigres' civil rights; and Great Britain was two-faced about them. London condemned flagrant abuses of Indian rights when Gandhi raised them to the world's attention, but at the same time secretly coached South African politicians. The white man did not want mercantile or professional Indians to be in this land. Nor did they want the Indian population plague to spread out of Natal once it became part of the Union of South Africa in 1910.

Through many years of South African Indian advocacy, even though he was sometimes jailed or abused, Mohandas K. Gandhi did not lose his faith in the ultimate rectitude of English law. In 1911, after eighteen years of struggle, he patiently restated the British subject's right to freedom: "The genius of the British constitution requires that every subject of the Crown should be free as any other, and, if he is not, it is his duty to demand and fight for his freedom so long as he does so without injuring anyone else."

Gandhi's commitment to constitutional ideals was unflinching. In 1897, as his ship docked, he was warned that speeches he had made during a visit to India had been distorted in the Natal press and were causing broad hostility toward him. The police wanted him to go ashore privately in darkness. Instead, he bravely walked into Durban beside a fair-minded English lawyer, F. A. Laughton, who was usually an opponent in court.

Gandhi was recognized, and the trailing crowd quickly became an ugly mob who separated the men, began pelting the unresisting Indian with debris, and soon were beating and slashing at him murderously. At this critical moment, Mrs. R. C. Alexander, wife of Durban's police chief, swinging her umbrella as a club, penetrated to the victim's side, and, in the stand-off, Gandhi survived. He brought no charges; his assailants were misinformed, he said, and should be left out for that reason.

Two years later Gandhi organized an Indian ambulance corps, in which he served, for the Boer War. The corp members were mentioned repeatedly in dispatches for valorous service under fire, rescuing wounded British soldiers on the battlefields, saving many white lives.

It was in his South African years that Gandhi visualized and began the technique he called *saty agraha:* nonviolent firmness showing the way of truth beyond error. In practice this meant breaking bad laws, without pride or rancor, and passively accepting punishment in whatever form it was delivered. South African authority learned that

Mohandas K. Gandhi as a young Indian civil rights advocate in Natal (1893).

Gandhi, when faced with choice between fines and imprisonment, chose the latter, often recommending to the judge that he order the maximum sentence! Gandhi in jail publicized British repression of Indians to international opinion.

Indian merchants and professionals wished to settle in Johannesburg, and some did, against fierce Afrikaner constraints: pass laws, business licensing to restricted areas, high taxes, easy deportation, tiny immigration quotas. Gandhi tirelessly campaigned against these discriminatory measures. He probed and negotiated for eight years with General Jan C. Smuts, the most cosmopolitan of the Afrikaner politicians. One of Smuts's associates—after Gandhi said he would not add to the government's burdens by mounting a protest during a railway strike—burst out:

> *I do not like your people, and do not care to assist them at all. But what can I do? You help us in our days of need. How can we lay hands on you? I often wish you took to violence like the English strikers, and then we would know at once how to dispose of you. But you will not injure even the enemy. You desire victory by self-suffering alone and never transgress your self-imposed limit of courtesy and chivalry. And that is what reduces us to sheer helplessness.*

Gandhi wound up his South African mission after an impressive show of strength: Over two thousand Indian coal miners, whom he had prompted to strike in protest of a head tax, were turned out penniless by the mine proprietors. Gandhi marched them into Transvaal illegally, where, as expected, all were arrested (and put onto government board). Gandhi and aides were placed in solitary confinement plus hard labor; the strikers returned to the mines (made extensions of the jails) and forced to labor under whip and pistol. But disturbances among Natal's 150,000 Indians almost became an insurrection. Abruptly Gandhi and friends were released, and the head tax was eventually ended. In protracted negotiations among Gandhi, Smuts, and London, the Indian minority seemed, on paper at least, to gain freedom close to that of white South Africans.

The resistance movement in India had been calling, and in 1914 Mohandas K. Gandhi sailed away. General Smuts's prayer—"The saint has left our shores. I sincerely hope forever."—was to be fulfilled.

The fix on Indian rights did not hold. Transvaal passed (1919) severe laws restricting individuals and companies. The Indian vote was denied (1924), and many occupations were closed to them (1926); land-ownership freezes and a forced move into ghettos came in the 1940s and 50s. Indians remain a modest minority in South Africa.

The incoming Liberal government in London was as anxious as its predecessor to keep South African mines producing. Self-government in the former Boer republics and then in the 1910 Union of South Africa (Cape Colony, Natal, the Orange Free State, Transvaal,) was entrusted to a pair of famed Boer generals of the late war. Prime Minister Louis Botha and right-hand associate, Jan C. Smuts, were judged politically safe Afrikaners, but their allegiance to the British Empire was soon sorely tested.

In 1914, World War I (Britain, France, Russia, and Italy, versus Germany, the Austrian Empire, Turkey) opened, and on the pledge by Prime Minister Botha of loyalty and military cooperation, British troops in South Africa were withdrawn to the homeland. The Boer War, with its terrible toll upon the Afrikaner civilian population, had ended just eleven years before, and bitterenders everywhere rejected loyalty to Britain, their former enemy. It would be better to aid Germany and later regain independence. So, when the Botha regime remained actively pro-British, there was a revolution in Transvaal and the Orange Free State.

General Christiaan De Wet, the foxiest of wartime commando leaders, gathered a force there with other unreconciled officers and was supported by thousands of conservative Afrikaners. However, Botha was still able to field thirty thousand Afrikaner soldiers (no English were used) willing to fight their ethnic kin, De Wet's fourteen thousand rebels. In a classic exchange, a village dame called out: "Where are the damned English?" and a Botha trooper replied: "*We* are the damned English, old woman!"

The government won out in a brief campaign, with only a few

hundred casualties on either side, and De Wet was jailed. General Botha went on to conquer German Southwest Africa (Namibia today), and General Smuts warred successfully in German East Africa (Tanzania). In these leaders Britain had chosen true and brave men who also foresaw international partnership as the best path toward independence. But the extremist Afrikaners had new grievances to feed their racist political philosophy. These eventually brought the Nationalist party to power.

Prime Minister Louis Botha died in 1919 and was succeeded by Jan C. Smuts. He, in 1922, had to deal summarily with a workers' revolt on the Rand. Postwar Europe's economic woes reached South Africa, where the wages paid to white miners were cut. A strike started among skilled white coal miners and soon spread into the Rand gold mines. There was strong suspicion that the mine owners were setting the stage to violate the status quo color bar; that is, to redistribute mine jobs to employ more of the poorly paid black workers. A rallying cry of the strikers was: "Are you for a white South Africa?"

Among the ugly outcomes of the Boer War had been the appearance of "the poor white problem." These were landless rural families who, because they were now unable, as in the past, to expand into a limitless veld, drifted to the cities and industrial centers. They were practically as unskilled for urban employment as the blacks from the reserves and *very touchy* about such comparisons.

They were whites who demanded their racial standard of living. So they were defensive about doing menial tasks; such "kaffir jobs" were proudly disdained as degrading. Their plight, added to their large numbers, attracted extremist Afrikaner politicians, so government policy was directed to keeping black standards and visibility below theirs. Many poor whites were eventually subsidized in make-work petty government positions—not economic, but if hardheaded capitalists would not employ them, the government could retrieve the subsidies in higher industrial taxes.

In 1922 there were plenty of poor whites to sign on as "scabs,"

Jan Smuts, cosmopolitan Afrikaner statesman for over half a century.

taking over the white mine jobs of the strikers. South African communists gained control of the strikers, organized armed worker commandos, and launched a revolt in the Rand.

The Smuts government quickly reacted and crushed the revolt with its army; two hundred thirty persons, mainly strikers, died. The strike was lost, but labor took political revenge by voting with the ultraconservative Afrikaners, whose party defeated Smuts in 1924 elections. The new regime, headed by Jan Hertzog, yet another ex-Boer general, set out upon a program to protect the white minority from top to bottom by dismantling any tokens of equality remaining to the black majority.

Out of the racial fears of small tradesmen and farmers, and of the partially redeemed poor white classes, there emerged during the Depression of the 1930s the Afrikaner Broederbond (Brotherhood), South Africa's most visible invisible white supremacy group. A secret league of picked activists pledged to infiltrate South Africa's organizations at every level, the Broederbond's mission was to protect and promote white dominance. The effort was successful, and the Broederbond endures into the present with an elite membership believed to be above twelve thousand, including most political, bureaucratic, and military personages.

The hard times of the 1930s brought back former premier Jan Christiaan Smuts. He returned in time to counteract the pro-Nazi feelings of the reactionaries who admired Hitler's ideas of racial purity. So, when World War II started in 1939, Smuts again was able to swing South Africa to Britain's side. The parliament vote was eighty to sixty-seven. One of three eligible men volunteered for the armed services. Also, seventy thousand (unarmed) blacks, and forty-five thousand colored and Indian support troops accompanied the nation's combat forces.

Jan Hertzog had resigned in protest after the pro-British war vote, and the conservative faction reacted by founding the Nationalist party. It was in 1944 that its leader, Dr. Daniel F. Malan, first talked about "apartheid." Dr. Malan promoted this idea of racial apartness as progress beyond "segregation." Under apartheid, he claimed, it would not be one race oppressing another, but a program determining each race's *separate* development. As a successful candidate in 1948, Dr. Malan directly addressed the worst white fears:

> *Will the European race in the future be able to maintain its rule, its purity and its civilization, or will it float along until it vanishes forever, without honor, in the black sea of South Africa's non-European population? . . .*

> *As a result of foreign influences, the demand for the removal of all color bars and segregation measures is being pressed more and more continuously and vehemently; and all this means nothing less than the white race will lose its ruling position and that South Africa will sooner or later have to take its place among the half-caste nations of the world.*

The foreign influences Dr. Malan complained of were recent, post–World War II. White rule of racial majorities was universal throughout the colonial (today called "Third World") lands through 1945 at least. It was widely believed that a century or two of cultural evolution must occur before the "colored" races would be fit to order their own destinies—and there was a lot of money to be made from "the white man's burden" before then! Benevolent gestures toward native populations were predominantly of the pat-on-the-head type.

Even in the United States, with its constitutional civil rights guarantees, nonwhite minorities were ignored or oppressed in 1948. The Indian Reservation system matched that of South Africa's Native Reserves. Uprooted American tribes had been pushed, sometimes thousands of miles, into wastelands of white choice and there forgotten, since their numbers were small, not worth exploiting economically. Also, a color bar discriminating against black Americans was broadly in place across the United States in 1948, and in the southlands rivaled the intensity of the South African racial code.

After the war, it seemed that in the vast colonial world stretching through Africa and southern Asia, self-determination by native peoples was possible because war-exhausted colonial powers were beset by the expansion of international communism. India/Pakistan showed the way to independence in 1947. The allure of *Uhuru!* (freedom) swept through colonial Africa in the following decades, turning out by negotiation and revolution the European masters who had ruled them since the previous century. By the 1970s, South Africa stood alone in its absolute white minority rule.

The dominant white tribe in South Africa had been rooted there for three hundred years and considered it absolutely their homeland. Unlike white Angolans, Kenyans, or Rhodesians, they had no mother country to retreat to. They were a proud, ingrown people who shunned outside influences and were not impressed by world opinion. Also, the Afrikaner was toughly self-reliant, and was as likely to share power willingly with other South African tribes as Shaka Zulu had been.

When Dr. Malan, raised to the premiership by white fears of black aspirations, preached in parliament that apartheid would tolerate no racial equality in white areas while allowing progress for the Africans within their Native Reserves, he did not easily handle hostile questions about how this would be achieved. But no matter; he had Dr. Hendrik Verwoerd, the energetic, self-confident Minister of Native Affairs available. And Verwoerd as chief apartheid technician provided all the answers.

Hendrik Verwoerd was born in Holland in 1904, but his middle-class family soon emigrated to the Cape Colony, where his father's part-time missionary work for the Dutch Reformed Church called him to a pastorate in Rhodesia. In the time of World War I, young Verwoerd's anti-British sympathies got him suspended by his English schoolmaster. The Verwoerd family then moved into the Afrikaner heartland of the Orange Free State. It was from there that Hendrik, a bright and tireless student, went on to Stellenbosch University in the Cape Colony, originally to train for the ministry,

Apartheid's planners at a Nationalist Party conference: (right to left) *Daniel F. Malan, J. G. Strijdom, and Hendrik F. Verwoerd.*

but shifted into the study of psychology. Deciding to become a scholar in that field, Verwoerd sailed to Germany for postgraduate studies.

Germany in the late 1920s was an inflation-wracked land seeking a leader to take it out of its economic and political dilemmas. Adolf Hitler's Nazi party was coming on strong. In times of trouble, a universal scapegoat is a favored political ploy. Hitler chose the Jews. The twenty-four-year-old psychology student listened, and returned to South Africa imbued with the lore of racial purity and the necessity of watchful anti-Semitism. The Broederbond took him in and by the late 1930s, he was a political journal editor for the extremist Afrikaners, who coalesced as the Nationalist party after Smuts took South Africa into World War II. In those years Verwoerd narrowly managed to keep his editorializing above treason—he said one could admire Nazi ideals without approving their methods or the war.

When Dr. Hendrik Verwoerd received the post of Minister of Native Affairs in the Malan government, he was delighted. This powerful position carried the potential of controlling every phase of the lives of the colored four-fifths of South Africa's population, an opportunity Verwoerd yearned for. He had turned out a handsome, smooth personality with a talent, rare in Afrikanerland, for manipulating public relations. Beneath the self-assurance lay ruthless, inflexible attention to the policy of apartheid.

In 1950, when assuming the direction of native affairs, he assured white South Africa that he remained their man: "[I would not] do anything in the interests of the Bantus at the expense of the whites, because I would not take up a spade to turn the first sod in digging the grave of the white man." By contrast, soon a hymn in the African's vernacular was circulating in the Native Reserves. Its refrain is summarized in the last stanza:

> *Dr. Verwoerd, thou art with us!*
> *Glory unto thee our redeemer,*
> *Praises be unto Dr. Verwoerd,*
> *The defender of the Bantu,*
> *He that helped the chiefs by giving them good laws,*
> *He that gave our schools proper education,*
> *Because he knew what we needed*
> *And what we could not manage.*

11

Apartheid Induces Black Backlash

For fifty years, native African civil-rights activists demanded equality before the English law. Like Gandhi, they held a great respect and faith, which was long in dying, for the ultimate right of the English system.

In the twentieth century, official English civil rights attitudes were overshadowed by economic interest in an industrialized South Africa thriving on its cheap, depressed native labor. Also, British authority over South African affairs became increasingly irrelevant as imperial power waned during the two world wars. Home-grown white Afrikaners, rising in power, were absolute unbelievers in native African civil rights.

The African National Congress (ANC), long-time rallying organization of black-civil-rights activism, was formed in 1912. During its first forty-plus years of peaceable activity, it persistently sent delegations to confront governments at home and abroad with reasonable requests for civil justice, and publicized as broadly as possible the plight of nonwhite South Africans. For these efforts it received sympathy and some aid from white liberals at home and internationally. No progress in easing the practice of economic and social discrimination occurred; instead, white dominance swelled. Black trade unionism fared poorly, too; an attempt at a landmark strike in

1946 was harshly suppressed by the moderate Smuts government.

A revolution in tactics began from the 1950s, accelerating to the black rage at Soweto in 1976. At this time, the rest of Africa was turning out its white colonial masters and beginning to rule itself, offering by example a distant hope for Africans bowed beneath Afrikanerdom. However, the main reason the blacks hardened their style of confrontation was and is the black backlash against the rigid and demeaning set of strictures generally called apartheid.

Hendrik Verwoerd promoted his brainchild as a step into the future, a dynamic movement past the stagnation in segregation that was part of South Africa's social fabric from the arrival of the whites. Under apartheid, it was claimed, each race would fulfill its capacity and destiny *separately* (as God intended). But Verwoerd did not intend to divide the land into equally independent, healthy, self-sustaining white and nonwhite nations. The high white standard of living depended upon the availability of cheap African labor. The laws of apartheid tightened control over the supply and mobility of that labor, while warehousing the majority population in "independent" tribal reserves, out of white sight and mind when the Africans were not performing prescribed tasks on behalf of the whites in urban black townships.

Apartheid was partly window-dressing to placate outside opinion, but principally a guarantor and purifier of white dominance. In the 1950s, new restrictive laws flowed out of the Afrikaner-dominated legislature, shaping the face and force of apartheid.

Afrikaner administrators needed to know who was who; therefore, an early law was the Population Registration Act. People had to be classified by the government as white, native, or colored and issued an identity card. Persons displeased with the decision might appeal to a government board. "Colored" were later subdivided as Chinese, Indians, Malays, and other Asiatics outside the mixed-race group called Cape Coloured. The Prohibition of Mixed Marriages Act and an Immorality Act, each with stringent penalties, shut down legal sexual contacts between races.

To Verwoerdian separatists, racial residence was a crucial factor. At the coming of industrialization employing cheap African labor, and a matching demand for servants in support of the whites, segregated shanty villages had arisen adjacent to white towns. Under apartheid these picturesque and squalid barrios were to be displaced. New, drab but hygienically improved housing was raised in locations well away from white habitations. Sometimes their names were bureaucratically cheerless; Soweto is slang for Southwest Township.

The layout of townships, combined with their isolation, are a policeman's dream. Anyone coming or leaving can be efficiently monitored. There are no crooked alleys or hidden assembly points. Minor or major civil disturbance can be restricted to the African township without inconvenience to (or even knowledge of) the white residents living over the horizon in their towns. The Group Areas Act enabled this.

The new urban residences were also the setting for attempted reintegration of African tribal descendants. Verwoerd set out to divide the black people. Each black must be identified with his tribe. Tribal segregation was arranged within the African location whenever possible, and tribal togetherness encouraged. In this way the whites hoped to slow black intertribal unity against them.

Conservative Afrikaners believed they could never include non-whites in national citizenship. Verwoerd, in introducing his "Bantustans," native independencies, sought to legalize the foreign character of South Africa's majority peoples. Eight, later ten, often-fragmented areas containing below twenty percent of South Africa's area became homelands to above eighty percent of the population. Black tribal nationalities were called Kwazulu, Swazi, Qwaqwa, and Transkeian. Each "nation" was promoted as "ruling itself" under white-appointed blacks, with an ultimate white veto reserved as necessary.

Typically, the new homelands were overcrowded former Native Reserves on indifferent or abused agricultural lands unable to sustain their populations. Some financing to establish African business or improvements (Bantu Investment Corporation Act) was promised but was very slow in coming from the Afrikaner government. It would not be to the advantage of the government if the new puppet independencies became very prosperous. White South Africa still needed their labor, especially that of persons forced by dire circumstances to accept any job at a low wage. And now that the Bantu had been changed into foreign migrants by Verwoerd's laws, they became guest laborers without claim to inherent rights: persons easily handled, shifted about, and deported if unemployed, sick, elderly, or troublemakers.

In the area of labor relations there wasn't much that the lawmakers of apartheid could improve upon their predecessors. They had long since installed effective Job Reservation Laws, dividing white and nonwhite occupations. And wages had been kept in hand; during one twenty-year stretch, black mine wages had not been raised a shilling! Verwoerd did implement the Settlement of Disputes Law, which forbade strikes or negotiations by Africans or their unions. Workers were to submit their grievances to one of those familiar nonresponsive government boards.

With intent to assure that future generations of workers be properly groomed and suitably docile, the Bantu Education Act was passed. The government undertook all black education. There would be much more of it, a better school plant and staffing, but the government prescribed the substance and level of it, usually preparation for a lifetime of manual labor: "He must not be subject to a school system which draws him away from his own community," specified Dr. Verwoerd, "and misleads him by showing him the green pastures of European society where he is not allowed to graze." Nonwhites were barred from attending white universities, but might attend their own, when and where they were established.

The so-called petty apartheid laws were gathered into the Preservation of Separate Amenities Act, which set up the necessity of racially divided facilities in public accomodations: beaches, benches, toilets, transportation, and at all sports or entertainment occasions. The white/nonwhite separation even applied to service windows in banks and post offices. (Such facilities were also then common in sections of the United States)

The Pass Laws insured that the repressed majority did not evade the white system. They had been in force since the first significant mingling of the races. By the 1950s an urban African needed several bits of official paper to justify job, residence, and ethnic origin. Hendrik Verwoerd undertook to fool outsiders when he called his law on this subject the Abolition of Passes and Coordination of Documents Act. Now each nonwhite was required to carry only one biographical reference booklet. But it contained all personal records as it interested the government, and included his/her photograph and fingerprints. Another section informed the holder of limitations and responsibilities.

The Nationalist administration equipped itself legally to deal arbitrarily with transgressors of apartheid. The Suppression of Communism Act, broadly worded and used, was the first in an expanding series of laws allowing unusual search, seizure, and detention procedures. Under the later Terrorism Act, "causing feelings of hostility between Whites and Blacks" was sufficient cause to allow arrest and long, isolated detention before the trial process.

This summary roll of apartheid's structures could be administered only by a police state. For a few paragraphs, try to visualize *yourself* as subject to apartheid:

Born into a large, poor family in a Bantustan made out of a crowded African Reserve, you have absorbed a few years education offered by the government; this includes conditioning instruction about your place in life and why you must be satisfied while hopeful, for your black and white overseers are working together to improve conditions. Soon it is necessary to obtain a job and aid your family as it struggles at subsistence level. There are no jobs in your neighborhood, but fortunately the white man wants your labor in a distant city. It seems an adventurous opportunity, for even though you are young and green, you sense that your birthplace is a backwater of failure.

The first glimpses of the white man's city are exciting, marvelous; but they remain glimpses from the window of the bus that carries you daily on the long haul between the isolated township, where you lodge with others from your area, and the job. You do simple, repetitive work on the assembly line in an appliance factory. It's dull, and there is no apparent chance of job improvement. Well, at least you are drawing a wage and have food and a bed. There is little variety to free time, either, for you are restricted to your living place.

The whites you encounter are supervisors at the factory who, if they take notice at all, treat you like a commodity. There is also contact with the police, black and white, who frequently comb the township where you live. "Kaffir! Let's see your pass." How many times have you heard that? Dozens! And usually in a most demeaning, unfriendly tone.

Then one day the white man tells you that you are no longer to work in the factory or the city. You are going to live on a melon farm and draw a smaller wage. You protest respectfully. The white man looks through you and curtly announces: "Next." On the melon farm it goes badly. You do not care for stoop labor, nor for the grouchy tyrant who owns the farm. So one night, fed up, you run away back to the city and enter the substratum of blacks that exists on a catch-as-catch-can footing. You hear, generally for the first time, outspoken criticism of the white man and his system and are told the lore of revolution.

But, unadept newcomer as you are, soon comes the day when: "Hey, kaffir; stop where you are! Show us your pass" takes you out of circulation. You vow that even the jail is better than that melon farm! Eventually you are returned to your Bantustan. The black police there will watch you as a troublemaker; and it is doubtful whether you can again find work. To the white man, you are a soiled commodity who must be cleansed before ever you can labor again for him, even on a melon farm. Your future is as grim as the present.

Organized resistance arose as the discriminatory apartheid laws were handed down. In 1952, to emphasize a call for their repeal, the

"Kaffir! Show me your pass."

African National Congress mounted a "defiance campaign" that involved nonviolent civil disobedience, mainly of petty apartheid ordinances. This period is identified with Albert Luthuli, a well-educated Zulu chieftan and ANC district leader who was forced out of tribal office by the government for supporting the campaign. He promptly became the charismatic chief of the ANC, declaring:

> *Who will deny that thirty years of my life have been spent working in vain, patiently, moderately and modestly at a*

*closed and barred door? What have been the fruits of modera-
tion? The past thirty years have seen the greatest number of
laws restricting our rights and progress until today we have
reached a stage where we have almost no rights at all.*

However, Luthuli, fifty-five, had been raised in and practiced a
staunch Christianity. He remained opposed to violence or revolution
and was the last of the predominantly hopeful African leaders:

*Our situation in the Union may be grim, but it is not hope-
less. There is still enough goodwill and charitableness among
South Africans, Black and White, if only the leaders, both
Black and White, and the government would get together to
talk things over.*

The Nationalist party government didn't talk it over with Albert
Luthuli. They banned his public speaking and set out to suppress
peaceful civil disobedience by police methods. Up to eight thousand
protesters were arrested. Special laws threatened lengthy prison
terms, and the ready application of whips was sanctioned. The
Defiance Campaign was stopped.

Although under some form of government restraint on public
actions for the rest of his life, Luthuli, in the 1950s, remained the
African's principal spokesman and ANC leader. He worked coopera-
tively with the Indian minority, the Cape Coloured people, and the
liberal white South African dissenters. In 1956, the government, on
bad legal advice, attempted to jail partisans of all these factions on
an overall charge of "treason" (Suppression of Communism Act).
Luthuli and his deputy, Nelson Mandela, were among the 156
activists arrested. The case aroused worldwide moral and financial
support for the accused. The lawyers for the defense argued brilliantly; the state persisted stubbornly in its charge. After five years
in South African courts, all the accused in the case (long freed on
bail) were acquitted because: (1) their adherence to communism was

not shown and (2) they had not conspired to overthrow the govern-ment.

In 1960 the African National Congress laid plans for another landmark peaceable civil disobedience campaign. This would be against the Pass Laws (now also having been extended to women). Albert Luthuli spoke passionately:

> *Without a pass, an African is worse than emasculated. Without a pass he has no right to work, to travel, to walk up a street, even to be alone at home. . . .*

> *The fear of a loud, rude bang on the door in the middle of the night, the bitter humiliation of an undignified search, the shame of husband and wife huddled out of bed in front of their children by the police and taken off to a police cell . . .*

> *South Africa for the African is a vast series of displaced person camps. Individuals are shuffled around. Whole towns of thousands of people are lifted up . . . and thrown down elsewhere. . . .*

> *Each year half a million of my people are arrested under the Pass Laws.*

It was at this time that a younger, more aggressive section of the ANC, which wanted to cut ties with all nonblack associates of the resistance, split off as the Pan Africanist Congress, led by Robert Sobukwe. The PAC took over the pass campaign by mounting one of their own ten days ahead of the ANC's date. African men were instructed to converge on their district police stations and turn in their passes.

During the event on March 21, 1960, nervous and/or arrogant police opened fire on an approaching crowd in the Sharpeville township, south of Johannesburg. The African death toll—most were shot in the back in this massacre—was sixty-seven killed and 186 wounded. The same day, in a pass protest that turned into a battle, police shot two Africans dead and injured forty-nine, at Langa, near Capetown.

After these tragedies, it took courage for the ANC to proceed with its own Pass Law defiance. However, Chief Luthuli stepped out and publicly burned his pass, as did thousands. The alarmed government arrested Luthuli and others, outlawing the ANC completely. Because of illness, the ANC chief was let out of a jail term; instead he was put under tight house arrest at a rural location.

But the steadfast apostle of nonviolence was not yet silenced. The Nobel Peace Prize for 1960 was awarded to Albert Luthuli, and a chagrined South African government allowed him just ten days out of their grip to go to Norway and return with his honors. In accepting the prize, a portion of the speech by the venerable champion of African rights defined their extent:

In government we will not be satisfied with anything less than direct individual adult suffrage and the right to stand for and be elected to all organs of government.

In economic matters we will be satisfied with nothing less than equality of opportunity in every sphere, and the enjoyment of all of those heritages which form the resources of the country which up to now have been appropriated on a racial "whites only" basis.

In culture we will be satisfied with nothing less than the opening of all doors of learning in non-segregatory institutions on the sole criterion of ability.

In the social sphere we will be satisfied with nothing less than the abolition of all racial bars.

Under house arrest, Chief Albert Luthuli and family receive his Nobel Peace Prize nomination.

In 1961 Albert Luthuli passed on to the younger Nelson Mandela the leadership of the now illegal African National Congress. The winner of the Nobel Peace Prize continued in house arrest until his death in 1967.

Dr. Daniel Malan, who had put his Nationalist party into office, had retired and been replaced by J. G. Strijdom, a party hardliner who died in office. In 1958 it was Hendrik Verwoerd, apartheid's most enthusiastic strategist, who became prime minister. His ascent was a popular move at home in a time when apartheid had made South Africa unpopular abroad, including with Great Britain and the Commonwealth family nations. Dr. Verwoerd considered both factors and, in a political gamble, called for a vote on South African independence. The prime minister severed South African relations with England and took the country out of the multiracial, decidedly critical, Empire Commonwealth, too.

The suppressed African National Congress tried to generate an impressive protest show of strength on South Africa's Independence Day, but the demonstrations were poorly attended. Mandela and his ANC colleagues groped for strategy to regain the initiative against Verwoerd but found it difficult as an illegal organization unable to operate publicly.

Nelson Mandela, forty-three in 1961, came from princely stock in the Xhosa Bantu. He became a lawyer in Johannesburg, associated with another young man, Oliver Tambo (in the 1980s the ANC chief in exile). The firm of Mandela and Tambo busied itself with African civil and criminal cases, plentiful even in the 1940s, sometimes representing seven court cases simultaneously. Mandela's association with the ANC dated from those times. He became a popular and successful promoter of the organization's youth wing. A sparkling asset to Mandela's personal and professional well-being was and is Winnie Mandela, his second wife, whom he married in 1958, during the Treason Trial period. Her unwavering commitment and peppery style in public relations superbly bolstered her husband's resolute image in the long time of separation and imprisonment that stretched ahead.

Stymied publicly by the Verwoerd government, fearful that it might be forgotten, the ANC, with Mandela's approval, authorized its militant Spear of Africa partisans to keep in the public eye by sporadic acts of sabotage. This was a dubious choice. It gave the government justification to employ police emergency laws and actions, and to accuse the ANC of communist-backed terrorism. (The ANC accepts communist aid; Mandela denies communist leanings.) The destruction ANC sabotage caused was unimportant, but the heightened police attention and infiltration resulted in Mandela's capture in 1962. The next year, a tip to the police disclosed that the secret headquarters of the ANC were in suburban Johannesburg. Many administrative leaders were taken in the raid. The ANC's effectiveness was disrupted within South Africa for years to come.

At the well-publicized trial in 1964, Mandela admitted to planning the sabotage offensive, stating that it was because the government had shut down any opportunity for dialogue and prohibited any forum for peaceable demonstrations. Then, familiar with courtroom affairs, Nelson Mandela spoke brilliantly, reasonably, affectingly on the national racial crisis, his beliefs, goals, hopes, and fears. Unmoved, the court sentenced the ANC chief and several associates to life imprisonment. But Mandela's stature in and beyond Africa had been raised by his performance in court and in the prisons where he yet remains in his seventieth year.

The government realized it had a political martyr on its hands. Though often a subject of strategy discussion, the Nationalist administration has not to date been able to bring itself to order Mandela's unconditional release. In 1985, P. W. Botha, South Africa's president, made public a conditional offer of release: Mr. Mandela must not again violate South Africa's laws, and especially must unconditionally reject violence as a political instrument.

Mandela's rejection of these terms was suitably eloquent. Here are some of his remarks transmitted from the isolation of his cell:

> *I am not a violent man. My colleagues and I wrote in 1952 to Malan asking for a round table conference to find a solution to the problems of our country, but that was ignored.*

> *When Strijdom was in power, we made the same offer. Again it was ignored.*

African National Conference (ANC) leader Nelson Mandela has been imprisoned for over twenty years.

When Verwoerd was in power we asked for a National Convention for all the people of South Africa to decide on their future. This, too, was in vain.

It was only when all other forms of resistance were no longer open to us that we turned to armed struggle.

*Let Botha show that he is different to Malan, Strijdom, and
Verwoerd. Let him renounce violence. . . .*

*What freedom am I being offered while the organization of
my people remains banned? . . . when I may be arrested on
a pass offense? . . . to live my life as a family with my dear
wife who remains in banishment in Brandfort? . . . when I
must ask permission to live in an urban area? . . . when I need
a stamp in my pass to seek work? . . . when my very South
African citizenship is not respected?*

*Only free men can negotiate. Prisoners cannot enter in con-
tracts.*

For the white man, apartheid in the 1960s was a success economically and socially. The nonwhites were controlled to provide effective
labor and segregated out of sight when not working. By 1970, South
African whites were the most affluent group in the world! Even black
South African income had been increasing at six percent annually,
and it was tirelessly pointed out that they were the wealthiest natives
in all of Africa. Their education was the best, too, despite only one
dollar spent for each ten dollars on white pupils. Hendrik Verwoerd
himself did not live past this period of peaking indicators. In 1966,
seated at his desk in the national parliament, he was attacked and
stabbed to death. The assailant was not an apartheid-crazed African;
Verwoerd's killer was a deranged white parliament employee who
said his giant (imaginary) tapeworm drove him to murder.

In the late 1960s labor shortages prompted some opening of
closed job categories, mostly to the Cape Coloured. Instances of
wage equalization startled the status quo: For example, Barclays
Bank (English) adjusted the discrepancy in wages, which had averaged $112 to nonwhite employees, $500 to the whites. When, after
agitation, the Johannesburg Health Department paid African physi-
cians the same fee scale as whites, the income of the former was

boosted three hundred percent. A slight right to strike was granted to nonwhites. In order to remain invited to international competitions, the state allowed some relaxation of sports apartheid.

Racial harmony was not achieved. Though the ANC was mainly in exile now, many local resistance bands formed but their careers were short. Disturbances arising from apartheid's injustices and militant labor agitation continued to pepper society. Police with whips and dogs responded as stolidly and efficiently as ever. The average white chose to ignore the roots of black despair and, unattended, it became violent.

12

Soweto: Youth's Black Rage

The post-war years saw the emergence of South Africa as a highly industrialized society with Johannesburg as the dynamic hub. To meet the labour demands of industry and commerce, the influx to the towns became a raging torrent of humanity and overwhelmed the meagre housing resources of the city at that time. As a consequence vast slums, with concomitant evils sprung up in and around Johannesburg.

The City Council had the responsibility of rehousing hundreds of thousands of Bantu working in its area, and the last two decades have seen the provision of liveable accommodation which was a complete break from the anti-social conditions of the past. In addition to the houses, services and amenities had to be provided.

In creating the multi-faceted entity which is Soweto, the Council has helped in one of the world's greatest slum clearance schemes of the post-war era.

As this public relations brochure tells it, initially the local authorities concerned with implementing Verwoerd's Group Areas Act were proud of Soweto, the showcase conglomeration of native townships southwest of Johannesburg, rebuilt into a vast, efficient Bantu residential holding area. About sixty thousand plain, serviceable, small houses (two bedrooms, outside flush toilet and water tap; rent, fifteen dollars a month) had been recently raised to accommodate up to half a million of Johannesburg's "guest laborers" and their families. Eventually one hundred thousand units would be built. White pride in apartheid's drawing-board dreams had even prompted the suggestion that the creation be named "Hendrik Verwoerdville."

Browsing on in the government's Soweto pamphlet (1970), with its color shots of contented black residents, a casual overseas reader could be impressed that though the Afrikaners were oppressing the natives' civil rights, they were certainly helping them out in a material way. Beyond the new housing, the urban planners had showered Soweto with white amenities: over 120 schools, 6 public libraries, 45 nursery schools, 7 clinics and a large hospital (fees: 50¢ for hospitalization, 20¢ for outpatient treatment). There were about 60 social clubs, many beer gardens and off-sale depots dispensing the mild Bantu beer and hard liquor as well. Health and fitness through sports were emphasized by 3 stadiums, 90 playing fields, 40 tennis courts, 4 swimming pools, 2 golf courses, along with 40 children's playgrounds.

Efficient commuter rail carried the adults to and from their jobs in Johannesburg. Businessmen and members of professions in Soweto were blacks, like their customers. There was black local government (white overseers held arbitrary authority). From their perspective, apartheid's planners had laid out Soweto to be as close to heaven as its denizens would likely ever get.

Yet, several years later, in 1976, Soweto erupted in civil insurrection, smoke, flames, and casualties. Apartheid's prize settlement had been allowed to become badly overcrowded. In 1976, Soweto may have held a million, or a million and a half; no one knew. Economic conditions in the far-off Bantustans remained unimproved. Their inhabitants believed that the only chance to get ahead lay in the cities. And the movement of the black population to the cities overwhelmed pass-law enforcement. Jan C. Smuts's prediction is well remembered in South Africa: "You might as well try to sweep back the ocean with a broom."

Overcrowding brought back into Soweto the "concomitant evils" the planners sought to exorcise. Overloaded local authority became ineffective. Municipal corruption swelled. High unemployment among the fugitives boosted the crime rate. A criminal subgovernment of the streets were the *tsotsis;* young men in mod costumes, who were amoral and very dangerous. A thin, lethal wire sliced between the ribs was a favored tactic. The alarming growth of social ills in Soweto mostly generated shrugs in white Johannesburg ten miles away: Well, what can you expect of kaffirs, anyway?

Apartheid, the constant shredder of innate human dignity, caused psychological abuse. The adult generation in Soweto buried its resentment in rationalization and forgetting. Alcoholism plagued the township. The elders had been beaten by the system.

From the mid-1960s, government control had forced a lull in African political activity. Beginning about 1970, inspired by similar groups in the United States, the Black Consciousness Movement was started by university-level students, of whom Steve Biko would become a future martyr. Racial pride had to be installed as the foundation stone for future racial greatness. Black power—we are strong and we are many—became the dream of African youth; the raised and thrust fist became the requisite greeting among aspiring blacks. Attitudes of black consciousness and power spread to younger groups, including those living in Soweto.

Young Africans had not yet been abased by the endless exploitation the whites laid upon their parents. They yearned to change the system during their lifetime and were groping for an issue or incident to serve as a catalyst. They were better informed than their elders; they had learned rather more than the Bantu Education Act had intended. Teenagers knew about the national liberations other black Africans had secured; they had some knowledge of the civil-rights struggles in the United States; they were aware of the communist aid and comfort given to black South African militants.

Black education in Soweto was neither compulsory nor free. So the few thousands who persevered into high school were the "best and brightest" in the townships, those who would make a difference in the future, if that were possible. And, then, in early 1976 the government handed them the rallying issue they had been seeking.

Lodged in the Bantu Education Act since its passage in 1955 was a provision that black education, traditionally taught in English, be given in Afrikaans as well. This provision had not been carried out. Now a new director of black education, Andries Treurnicht, pushed for compliance. It would start in the high schools in the southern Transvaal, including Soweto.

The Afrikaans curriculum was a hassle to all concerned. Typically, students absorbed their tribal language at home, then learned English in the schoolroom. Now they would have to learn Afrikaans as well. Many of their instructors were unable to teach in the language, and Afrikaans was the hated tongue of apartheid's enforcers; police had rudely shouted it at their parents in Soweto from the time of the children's first understanding: "Kaffir, waar's jou pas?" ("Nigger, where's your pass?")

Here was youth's black political consciousness rallying issue! Demonstrations arose, then school boycotts, then marches. As the atmosphere heated—a police lieutenant questioning students at a high school was threatened, saw his automobile burned, was rescued by a squad spreading tear gas—worried educators pointed out the potential for violent confrontation. One said that pushing the Afrikaans ordinance was like waving a torch beside a dry haystack. The Afrikaner bureaucrats were not impressed: They could go back to the reserves for "English" schooling; or they could just stay home.

Wednesday, June 16, 1976: A chilly winter smog overlays Soweto, but enthusiasm and anticipation is building in the streets. Boys and girls in neat school uniforms are greeting each other with raised fists: "Amandla Awethu!" ("Power to the people!"). They are not going to classrooms. Word has been passed (and peer attendance is mandatory) of a major anti-Afrikaans meeting in a football stadium. Students and hangers-on, estimated at up to twenty thousand, funnel by way of major avenues to the rally. Some carry outspoken placards; one calls upon Balthazar John Vorster, current premier: "If we must do Afrikaans, Vorster must do Zulu!"

So remote are police from the real Soweto that they are unaware of this gathering until marching columns are forming. Reacting in haste, ill-equipped at the scene, ten vanloads of police (about fifty men, of whom eight are whites, and two dogs) rush to confront a marching stream of young people. They are to disperse; they have not secured a permit. The police officer in charge, Colonel Kleingeld, seeks to so advise the marchers, but has no bull horn amplifier and is not heard. No police-to-people communication follows.

A shower of stones from the students is met by hurled tear-gas canisters, most of which do not explode. The crowd is raging now and does not flee before club-swinging police charge. The dogs are killed. A hail of stones beats upon the police from the sides as well as the front. Shots fired into the sky have no effect. The inadequate knot of police is menaced by hundreds on three sides. A bullet fired into the crowd of students kills thirteen-year-old Hector Petersen, Soweto's first black casualty. The police continue to fire and the crowd disperses.

But the students are not beaten down. They rage through Soweto's side streets, screaming out the shocking, infuriating news, accumulating recruits. *Tsotsis* thugs, who see an opportunity for breaking and entering unhindered, join the insurrection. Destruction, especially burning anything affiliated with government, begins. Targets include schools, offices, automobiles, state beer depots (the *tsotsis* concentrate on liquor shops); even a golf clubhouse is burning. Ominous black smoke plumes, visible in Johannesburg, rise above Soweto. It's open season on solitary whites—a municipal employee and a sociologist are stabbed or beaten to death. The sociologist had written a book on behalf of Soweto's distressed

Two students carry the body of another who was killed in the Soweto uprising. AP/WIDE WORLD PHOTO

youths. A white woman is able to escape by convincing a youth gang that she is English.

Police and student clashes resume as armored patrol vehicles ("hippos") roam turbulent Soweto. Sometimes hippos are halted by the press of surging masses attempting to injure the occupants, and the police shoot and ram a way out. The police fire randomly at streetside youths flexing fists in black power salutes. In the evening, anxious, bewildered parents return from their jobs in the city to meet civil rioters, whom they had left that morning as ordinary schoolchildren.

These scenes were repeated for three to four days before subsiding under police pressure. The first week's death toll was officially 176, all black but two. The residents of the embattled townships believed passionately that many more had died.

Confrontation and violence, instigated by young people, spread across South Africa in 1976. In the two months following the Soweto eruption, some eighty black communities experienced civil strife, and the unrest went on into and through 1977. Official government casualty figures for the entire Soweto-related period of violence list 3,907 injured, 575 killed. The latter figure is disputed by African veterans as being short by half or more.

Thousands were jailed. Though the government soon gave way on its Afrikaans language project, its response to the uprisings was harsher repression. To avoid arrest, thousands of bright young Africans fled their homeland; many became recruits in the communist-backed ANC armies in training over the border in neighboring Black Nationalist countries, but ideology for them took second place to their racial mission: "We are so fed up with apartheid," declared a student activist, "we would rather have communism." Meanwhile, the Afrikaner government suppressed the Black Consciousness organization, whose leader, Steve Biko, was beaten in a prison and callously allowed to die of his injuries.

In August 1976, the organizers of the fateful June rally formed the Soweto Student's Representative Council. It became an underground government in the chaos of the ravaged townships. The SSRC engineered more demonstrations, boycotts, and a Bantu strike that nearly paralyzed Johannesburg for a few days. Student activists also worked to involve adults, for example, the Black Parents Association. Winnie Mandela said that children had "risen and fought battles on behalf of their elders. . . . We know what we want. Our aspirations are dear to us. We are not *asking* for majority rule; it is our right, we shall have it at any cost."

Support came from white students at the Witwatersrand University, who marched under a banner that read DON'T START THE REVOLUTION WITHOUT US!, until they were assaulted by an Afrikaner crowd swinging chains and crowbars. The 1976 SSRC view of "Bantu Education" was scathing:

> *We shall reject the whole system of Bantu Education, whose aim is to reduce us, mentally and physically, into "hewers of wood and drawers of water" for the white racist masters.*

> *Twenty years ago, when Bantu Education was introduced, our fathers said: "Half a loaf is better than no loaf." But we say: "Half a gram of poison is just as killing as the whole gram."*

That's why so many schools were burned during youth's black rage in Soweto.

The younger generation of Africans segregated in or outside the white cities has been politicized by Soweto's racial upheaval and the many other disturbances that followed it into the 1980s. This advancement of political awareness can't be swept back by any white man's broom.

AFTERWORD

The Road Ahead?

The three-hundred-year-long road of South African racial relations crossed a great divide of national consciousness at the time of Soweto and related upheavals. The sense of political and social change approaching—so long delayed, and recently frustrated by the harsh application of apartheid by the traditional ruling but minority race— is now anticipated as a certainty by the nonwhite portion of the populace, which is expected to be nine out of ten of its citizens in the twenty-first century. In a very-best scenario, long-dominant white leaders will sit down with leaders of the black underclass to negotiate a relaxation of their exclusive rule. A consensus government of all South Africans would arise, a class structure based on ability replacing one stratified by racial origin.

But if such a benign and progressive solution is to occur, there will have to be an end to extremism; political and social extremism has for long been the most visible mover in South African affairs.

Whether the extremists can push the whites into a fateful confrontation with blacks depends on how the Africans (and their extremists) maneuver. The government has been spending thirty-five percent of its resources on security and has planned a national resistance for whatever comes. In open fighting it can defeat any presently conceived African force. Outsiders have little influence on the Afrikaner mind or actions. The bitterender tradition is well rooted, and the white tribe has no homeland other than South Africa.

After the Soweto period, the African militants were euphoric. They believed they would win in their lifetime. In the 1980s the various militant factions are quarreling among themselves. Intra-African warfare has wracked the rise of many other African republics. In South Africa, the militant African National Congress remains the rallying organization. But it contains communists, and they are interested in a complete overturn of the state, not a negotiated settlement with capitalists. The ANC sends bomb squads into the nation, yet hangs back from a total commitment to war. South Africa's recent trend toward success in settling quarrels and normalizing relations with black nations on its borders may inhibit ANC's punch from abroad.

The Botha regime has eased black restrictions somewhat (with a new constitution in 1984) but in a state of emergency since the severe 1984–1985 unrest in politicized African townships, it has (1988) refused to meet with the ANC. An inside national African leader they'd like to talk and negotiate with is Chief Mangosuthu Gatsha Buthelezi, of the Zulu nation. Zulus continue as leaders among the Bantu masses, and Chief Buthelezi, sometime past, established Inkatha, a semisecret organization with 1.3 million members. Inkatha has been compared in method and scope to the Afrikaner's Broederbond. The chief is no potential puppet; he demands an end to apartheid and majority rule, like the other leaders, but perhaps not so vindictively. His stated demands far exceed what Botha can or would agree to, presently.

A serious casualty of the Soweto uprising has been education for black South African youth. For about a decade since, the emotional slogan "Liberation before Education" was widely enforced by school boycotters, who got tough on students seeking to continue in schools; and also intimidated teachers and destroyed school property. The number of nonwhite young people affected at any time was in the 300,000 range. In 1987, however, a belated back-to-school movement began under the maturer realization that skilled hands will be needed when participation in the governing process is negotiated or seized.

Among scholars clinging to the hope of a nonviolent solution of the racial problems, South Africa's healthy, expanding nonwhite labor unions are a black hope. They are more interested in economic improvement than in ideology; therefore, they are unwilling to save South Africa by destroying it. Since industry is eighty percent dependent upon cooperation by Africans, there is a powerful political lever available in selected work stoppages or national strikes. If it can be believed that even in South Africa, man's income and wealth are final determinants of policy, then Alan Keyes, speaking before Congress as assistant secretary of state, may be prophetic:

> *You ask me where the pressure comes from. It hasn't come from outside. You give yourselves too much credit. The black people of South Africa have been able to organize themselves to put effective pressure on the situation. . . . The white South African government will in the end yield, not because it wants to, but because the future for blacks and whites in South Africa will be impossible unless such negotiations occur. . . .*

But what if race does matter the most? Remember Dr. Malan's remarks in introducing apartheid:

> *Will the European race in the future be able to maintain its rule, its purity and its civilization, or will it float along until it vanishes forever, without honor, in the black sea of South Africa's non-European population?*

Given that threshold priority, a terrible fight seems in prospect. But, however—whenever—majority rule *will* come to South Africa's long-oppressed nonwhite population. A trenchant proverb of hope in that country is: "Time is longer than rope."

Sources

Most of the facts printed and interpreted in *Along the Road to Soweto* were obtained from material available at the Library of Congress. This great library, also the illustration source for this book, is one of the most inspiratory results of American taxpayer dollars.

There are many quotations in this book from firsthand observators. A list of attributions for those with length of a paragraph or more follows:

Page 14 Quoted in Joao de Barros: *History of the Portuguese Conquest of Asia* (1556)

Page 27 Quoted in M. S. Geen: *The Making of South Africa* (1958)

Pages 34–35 Narrative of Sir John Barrow: *An Account of Travels into the Interior of South Africa* (1801)

Page 48 Narrative of Henry Dugmore: *Reminiscences of an Albany Settler* (printed 1958)

Page 50 Narrative of Henry Fynn: *Diary of Henry Francis Fynn* (1833)

Page 52 Fynn

Page 58 Fynn

Pages 59–60 Fynn

Pages 67–68 Quoted in George E. Cory: *The Rise of South Africa* (1910)

Page 86   Quoted in John Milton: *The Edges of War* (1983)

Page 89   Narrative of William J. Morton: *South Africa Diamond Fields, and a Journey to the Mines* (1877)

Pages 90–91   Morton

Page 105   Narrative of Henry Hook: "How They Held Rorke's Drift," *The Royal Magazine,* February 1905

Page 112   Quoted in J. S. Marais: *The Fall of the Kruger Republic* (1960)

Pages 115–116   Quoted in Eric Rosenthal: *Gold! Gold! Gold!* (1970)

Page 119   Quoted in C. E. Vulliamey: *Outlanders* (1938)

Page 125   Quoted in Eversley M. G. Belfield: *The Boer War* (1975)

Pages 132–133   Quoted in Arthur C. Martin: *The Concentration Camps* (1957)

Page 137   Theophilus Schreiner: *The Afrikaner Bond* (1901)

Page 140   Quoted in Robert A. Huttenback: *Gandhi in South Africa* (1971)

Page 144   In Huttenback

Page 149   Quoted in Robert W. Peterson (Ed.): *South Africa and Apartheid* (1975)

Page 152   Quoted in Alexander Hepple: *Verwoerd* (1967)

Pages 159–160   Quoted in John Addison: *Apartheid* (1982)

Page 160   Quoted in Melville Harcourt: *Portraits of Destiny* (1966)

Page 161   In Harcourt

Page 162   Quoted in Edward Callan: *Albert Luthuli and the South African Race Conflict* (1962)

Pages 165–167   Quoted in Mary Benson: *Nelson Mandela* (1986)

Page 169   Non-European Affairs Department, City Council of Johannesburg: *Soweto: A City within a City* (1970)

Page 176   Quoted in John S. Kane-Berman: *Soweto: Black Revolt, White Reaction* (1978)

Page 179   Quoted in the *Washington Post,* September 17, 1987

For Further Reading

There is no lack of material about South Africa. For instance, the Library of Congress's great collection holds more than seven thousand books and pamphlets.

An informal list of suggested books follows. In most cases, extensive bibliographies are included in these selections.

As overall fact mines, refer to *The Oxford History of South Africa* (2 vols.), Monica Wilson, ed., (1971), and *South Africa: A Country Study*, Harold D. Nelson, ed., (1981). Other general histories: *A History of South Africa*, by Cornelius W. DeKiewit (1943), is a brilliant dissection. Read anything by DeKiewit! *500 Years of South African History*, C. F. Muller, ed., (1969), contains essays with a conservative, insular South African viewpoint. *Blood River*, by Barbara Villet (1982), is a highly readable, fondly critical exposition of the Afrikaners, past and present. *Southern Africa Since 1800*, by Donald DeNoon (1982), is urbanely topical into the 1980s.

A History of Africa South of the Sahara, by Donald L. Wiedner (1962), briskly introduces the continent's history. *Congo to Cape*, by Eric Axelson (1973), details Portuguese exploration. *BC—1795*, by Christopher Danziger (1979), is a well-illustrated popular introduction to South Africa. *Those in Bondage*, by Victor DeKock (1950, 1971), describes Cape slavery in depth, and *The Cape Co-*

loured People, by J. S. Marais (1939), is a standard historical reference.

The collision of the whites with the Bantu (Xhosa) is well reported militarily in *The Kaffir Wars 1779–1877,* by A. J. Smithers (1973), and socially in *The Edges of War,* by John Milton (1983). *The Voortrekkers,* by Johannes Meintjes (1973), is a meticulously researched account of the "Great Trek." The landmark volume on the Zulu, 1800–1910, is *The Washing of the Spears,* by Donald R. Morris (1966). Also see *The Zulu War,* by David Clammer (1973).

South Africa's bonanzas of wealth are depicted best in *The Diamond Diggers,* by Herbert Ivor (1966), and *The Gold Miners,* by Alan Cartwright (1962). *Gold! Gold! Gold!* by Eric Rosenthal (1970), is notable for gossipy verve and its U.S. slant. Rosenthal is readable in his many books on the area.

The time of the titans—Rhodes, Kruger, Lobengula—is lyrically told in *African Portraits,* by Stuart Cloete (1946, 1969); compare with *The Outlanders,* by C. E. Vulliamey (1938). *The Pace of the Ox,* by Marjorie Juta (1937), is an atmospheric biography of Paul Kruger. Among the many, many biographies of Cecil Rhodes, *Cecil Rhodes,* by John E. Flint (1974), seems competently cool in assessment. *The Battle of Majuba Hill,* by Oliver Ransford (1967), incisively details Britain's Transvaal disaster. Ransford writes often and well on Africa. A standard volume, *The Jameson Raid,* by Jean Van Der Poel (1951), reports on Rhodes's debacle and disgrace.

The Boer War, by James Barbary (1969), is a fine survey written for teen readers. Heavyweights on the subject include *The Boer War,* by Thomas Pakenham (1979), and *The Anglo-Boer War,* by Byron Farwell (1976). *Mafeking,* by Brian Gardner (1966), appears designed to deflate Colonel Baden-Powell to life size. *Botha, Smuts and South Africa,* by Basil Williams (1946), recounts South Africa's history up to World War II. *Gandhi in South Africa,* by Robert Huttenback (1971), is meticulous in detail.

Apartheid, John Addison (1982), surveys its subject on behalf of teen readers. *The Anatomy of South African Misery,* by Cornelius

W. DeKiewit (1956), is a memorable indictment of apartheid. Its chief administrator is well profiled with his policies in *Verwoerd,* by Alex Hepple (1967). See also *South Africa and Apartheid,* Facts on File (1969). *King Solomon's Mines Revisited,* by William Minter (1987), discusses big business and apartheid.

African patriots speak out in *Let My People Go,* by Albert Luthuli (1962); *No Easy Walk to Freedom,* Nelson Mandela (1965); and the posthumous *I Write What I Like,* by Steve Biko (1978). *Nelson Mandela,* by Mary Benson (1986), is Mandela's biography by a veteran profiler of the African resistance. *Mandela's Children,* by Ora Mendels (1987), traces anti-apartheid organizations from the 1960s.

White Man, We Want to Talk to You, Denis Herbstein (1979), tells of the Soweto eruption as it occurred. *Soweto,* by Peter Magubane (1978), presents the photographic record. See also *Soweto: Black Revolt, White Reaction,* by John Kane-Berman (1978).

South Africa in the 1980s is covered by newsman Graham Leach in *South Africa* (1986). The African National Conference's (ANC) military agenda is discussed in *Apartheid's Rebels,* by Stephen M. Davis (1987). A cautious prescription for the future is given in *South Africa Without Apartheid,* by Heribert Adams and Kogila Moodley (1986).

INDEX